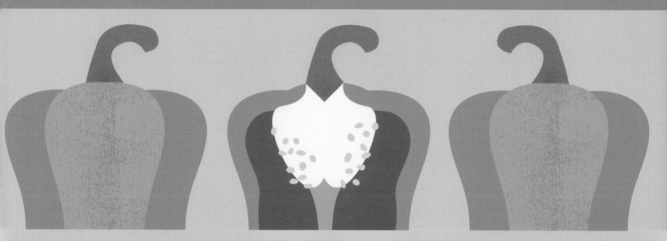

All my favourite foods but healthier versions!

DANIELLE

There is something for every day and for everyone!

JADE

The recipes have made me enjoy cooking so much

SUSAN

Easy to follow recipes that are delicious

SANDRA

Pinch

OF

Nom

EXPRESS

First published 2023 by Bluebird
an imprint of Pan Macmillan
The Smithson, 6 Briset Street, London EC1M 5NR
EU representative: Macmillan Publishers Ireland Ltd, 1st Floor,
The Liffey Trust Centre, 117–126 Sheriff Street Upper,
Dublin 1, D01 YC43

Associated companies throughout the world
www.panmacmillan.com

ISBN 978-1-5290-6228-1

3 5 7 9 8 6 4 2
A CIP catalogue record for this book is available from the British Library.
Printed and bound in Italy

Publisher Carole Tonkinson
Managing Editor Martha Burley
Project Editor Katy Denny
Production Manager Alenka Oblak
Art Direction Nikki Dupin and Emma Wells, Nic&Lou
Design Emma Wells, Nic&Lou
Illustration Shutterstock / Emma Wells
Photography Mike English assisted by Federica Cerniglia
Food Styling Kate Wesson assisted by Kristine Jakobssen
Prop Styling Max Robinson

Visit www.panmacmillan.com to read more about all our books
and to buy them. You will also find features, author interviews and
news of any author events, and you can sign up for e-newsletters
so that you're always first to hear about our new releases.

FAST, DELICIOUS FOOD

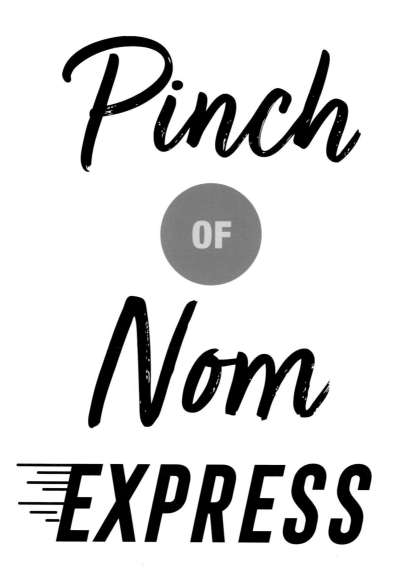

Pinch

OF

Nom

EXPRESS

bluebird
books for life

Kate *and* **Kay Allinson**

Contents

HELLO

Welcome to our latest book!

We feel incredibly lucky to be bringing you a brand-new cookbook, and we know that we owe it all to the wonderful Pinch of Nom community. When we sat down to plan *Express*, we spent a long time looking through your emails, messages and feedback, to make sure we built the recipes around what matters the most to you. With this in mind, we've created a collection of low-effort, big-flavour recipes that prioritise saving time in the kitchen, without compromising on enjoying healthy, home-cooked food. From meals that are on the table in a flash, to quick-prep recipes that can be left to do their thing in the oven, every dish in this book comes with our 'Express Promise'.

Our ultimate aim with this book is to put the trademark Pinch of Nom flavour on your table, with minimal disruption to your day. Inside these pages, you'll find all the familiar types of dishes that you're used to, with breakfast, fakeaways, snacks, sides and sweet treats covered. The big difference? This food comes with the 'Express Promise'. At its heart, this promise is all about making

good, nutritious, tasty meals that work around your day, your life and your family. That's why you'll find that we've separated out the recipes in the book into two main chapters: Quick Cook and Quick Prep.

When you need food on the table in a hurry, flick to the first chapter, where any of our Quick Cook recipes require less than 20 minutes of cooking time. Proving it doesn't take hours to create big flavours, turn to page 54 and simmer our Yellow Thai-style Curry for just 20 minutes. Plus, you won't want to miss the super speedy Garlic, Chilli and Parsley Spaghetti on page 58.

If you don't want to spend ages in the kitchen, but you don't mind leaving things to simmer, sizzle or roast, you're going to love the recipes we've saved for chapter two. The Quick Prep pages are brimming with dishes that take less than 15 minutes of peeling, chopping and assembling. We're talking about mouth-watering food like our Lemon and Ginger Chicken (page 134), Chimichurri Baked Cod (page 176) and Biscoff Sponge Traybake (page 206).

Just like in all our previous books, we've designed these recipes to only ever use simple ingredients and adapt to the equipment that you've already got in your kitchen. This is about making your life easier, after all! We've also added specific multi-method sections at the end of each chapter that include recipes for air fryers and slow cookers as well as more conventional cooking methods.

All that's left to say is thank you so much for being here for this book, no matter if you're new to Pinch of Nom, or you've been with us since the beginning. Whether it's a quick win for a midweek meal, a fast, flavourful fakeaway or a speedy, spur-of-the-moment dessert you need, we hope you turn to *Express* time and time again.

Kay x Kate

THE FOOD

As a classically trained chef, Kate has always loved recreating dishes and putting an original spin on classic recipes. This is how the very first Pinch of Nom recipes came to be, and it's this passion that means we can continue to bring fresh new flavours to you today. Kate and her small team of trusted recipe developers love nothing more than getting into the kitchen and experimenting with ingredients until some Pinch of Nom magic is created!

With these recipes, we wanted to show you that it's possible to create great-tasting food without spending all day prepping and cooking. To save time and unnecessary expense, we've kept things simple with fuss-free ingredients that you can use across multiple dishes. In fact, we'll only ever use an item that seems less common if it adds something really special to a dish – and even then, we'll try to make sure it's an ingredient that you can use more than once.

We take great care to make sure that the recipe methods suit any level of cooking skill, so even if you're a beginner in the kitchen, you'll have no trouble finding the time to prepare and cook slimming-friendly breakfasts, lunches, dinners and desserts.

While life moves fast, you're now armed with a cookbook chock-full of recipes that move faster – so it's far easier to say no to higher-calorie quick fixes! Wholesome, home-cooked food can take hours to prepare, or it can take minutes. With *Express* on your shelf, you'll always know that you can rustle up something delicious, on a timescale that works around your day.

As always, we've flagged vegetarian and vegan dishes, and added notes where ingredient swaps can be made. This'll help you spot the perfect recipe for the moment, even when you're flicking through in a hurry.

RECIPE TAGS

EVERYDAY LIGHT

These recipes can be used freely throughout the week. All the meals, including accompaniments, are under 400 calories. Or, in the case of sides, snacks and sweet treats, under 200 calories. Of course, if you're counting calories, you still need to keep an eye on the values, but these recipes should help you stay under your allowance.

WEEKLY INDULGENCE

These recipes are still low in calories, at between 400 and 500 calories, or 200–300 for sides, snacks and sweet treats, but should be saved for once or twice a week. Mix them into your Everyday Light recipes for variety.

SPECIAL OCCASION

These recipes are often lower in calories than their full-fat counterparts, but they need to be saved for a special occasion. This tag indicates any main meals that are over 500 calories, or over 300 for sides, snacks and sweet treats.

KCAL *and* CARB VALUES

All of our recipes have been worked out as complete meals, using standardised portion sizes for any accompaniments, as advised by the British Nutrition Foundation. Carb values are included for those who need to measure their intake.

GLUTEN-FREE RECIPES

We have marked gluten-free recipes with a GF icon. All these recipes are either free of gluten or we have suggested gluten-free ingredient swaps of common ingredients, such as stock cubes and Worcestershire sauce. Please check labelling to ensure the product you buy is gluten free.

FREEZABLE RECIPES

Look out for the 'Freezable' icon to indicate freezer-friendly dishes. The icon applies to the main dish only, not the suggested accompaniments.

All of these calculations and dietary indicators are for guidance only and are not to be taken as complete fact without checking ingredients and product labelling yourself.

KEY INGREDIENTS

PROTEIN

Lean meats are a great source of protein, providing essential nutrients and keeping you feeling full between meals. In all cases where meat is used in this book, we'd recommend using the leanest possible cuts and trimming off all visible fat. In many of our recipes you'll find that you can switch the type of protein for whatever meat you prefer. This especially applies to any mince recipes; minced turkey, beef or pork are easily interchangeable. Fish is also a great source of protein, and it's naturally low in fat. Fish provides nutrients that the body struggles to produce naturally, making it perfect for lots of our super-slimming recipes. And don't forget, vegetarian protein options can always be used instead of meat in all of the recipes in this book.

HERBS and SPICES

We love a bit of spice! One of the best ways to keep your food interesting when changing ingredients for lower-fat/sugar/calorie versions is to season it well with herbs and spices. In particular, mixed spice blends, either shop-bought or homemade, are perfect for certain recipes in this book, like our smoky BBQ Bolognese (page 166). Don't be shy with spices – not all of them burn your mouth off! We've added a spice-level icon to the recipes in this book, so you know what to expect. The beauty of cooking dishes yourself is you can always adjust the heat to your liking – add more or less chilli to suit. Always taste your food before adding extra spicing; this is particularly important if you're planning to double the quantities of sauce in a recipe. You'll often find that you don't need to double the amount of all the ingredients to achieve the right flavour – spices, vinegars, mustard and hot sauces should be added gradually, to taste.

STOCKS, SAUCES and THICKENERS

When you remove fat from a dish, flavours can dwindle. Adding spices is one way to boost flavours, but often the level of acidity in a recipe is much more important. When it comes to balancing and boosting flavours in our dishes, we love to use vinegar, soy sauce, fish sauce, Worcestershire sauce or Henderson's relish. One of Pinch of Nom's essential ingredients is the humble stock cube or stock pot; they add instant flavour and they're so versatile. We use various flavoured stock cubes and pots throughout this book, but there's always an option if you can't get your hands on the exact ones we've used. White wine stock pots, for example, can be tricky to find, but you can use 100ml of dry white wine and reduce the amount of water used in the recipe by 100ml instead (bear in mind this will add extra calories). It's worth noting that sauces, stock cubes and pots are often high in salt, so you may want to swap them for reduced-salt versions. Aside from being delicious with chips, reduced-sugar ketchup is also great for adding a rich depth of flavour to soups, stews or pasta sauces. A drizzle is all it takes to enhance the flavours on your plate, and the same is true of sweet chilli sauce. Use a dash to draw even more punchiness from our Zinger Tuna Fishcakes (page 230). From breakfasts to fakeaways, silky honey will give your cooking a touch of sweetness, without drying out your dish. It gives a gorgeous glaze to our Sticky Plum and Chicken Traybake (page 174).

We're often asked for tips on how to thicken soups, sauces and gravies. In the pre-slimming days, we wouldn't have thought twice about using a few tablespoons of flour to thicken liquids. Nowadays we're always on the lookout for lower-calorie and gluten-free options. Letting liquids reduce is a good way of thickening sauces without adding anything extra. As the moisture evaporates, the flavours get more concentrated too, so the end result will taste even better. You can also thicken recipes with potatoes (yes, really!). They're super starchy so they can be blitzed or mashed into your sauce or soup to soak up extra liquid. Bear in mind that this method will add some extra calories (1 large potato, about 369g, is about 311 kcal). A tomato-based dish such as tomato soup or bolognese can be thickened slightly using some tomato puree. This will add about 50 kcal per 51g tablespoon. You can use egg yolks or whole beaten eggs to thicken some soups and sauces. Drizzle a little of the hot liquid onto the egg, whisking vigorously, then stir the egg into the pan and heat gently until it thickens. 1 medium (57g) egg is about 76 kcal and 1 medium (18g) egg yolk is about 55 kcal. If making a roux-style sauce you can cut down on calories by making a slurry rather than using loads of butter. Simply mix your measured-out flour with a little water, then stir it into boiling liquid and simmer for a few minutes to cook the flour. 1 level tablespoon (20g) of plain flour is about 71 kcal. Another instant way to thicken any mixture is by using cornflour. This needs to be made into a slurry by mixing it with a little cold water and then adding this to the boiling liquid. Be sure to cook it until the starchy taste has gone. 1 level tablespoon of cornflour (20g) is about 69 kcal. It might be tempting to thicken stews or chillies with gravy granules, but this can add quite a few calories if you have a heavy hand. 1 teaspoon (5g) of gravy granules is about 21 kcal (depending on the brand). It's worth bearing in mind that gravy granules can also be high in salt.

REDUCED-FAT DAIRY

Substituting high-fat dairy products with clever alternatives can make a dish instantly lower in calories. You'll find that we'll often use reduced-fat cream cheese or spreadable cheese rather than the higher-fat versions.

TINS

Don't be afraid to bulk-buy tinned essentials! Beans, tomatoes and sweetcorn all come in handy time and time again. We often use them to add texture and flavour to stews, soups and salads. Using tinned ingredients can really help to keep costs down, and you'll never know the difference – used in these sorts of recipes they'll taste just as good as their fresh counterparts.

FROZEN FRUIT *and* VEG

Frozen fruit and veg make great filler ingredients and are perfect low-cost alternatives for recipes such as stews, where fresh ingredients aren't always necessary. Most of the time they're already peeled and chopped too, so they save time as well as money; you can just throw them in alongside your other ingredients.

PULSES, RICE *and* BEANS

High in both protein and fibre, keeping a few tins of beans and pulses in the cupboard is never going to do any harm! Rice is a fantastic filler and a great accompaniment to so many Pinch of Nom recipes.

BREAD, WRAPS *and* PASTRY

A great source of fibre, wholemeal bread is filling and versatile too – use it by the slice, or whizz it into breadcrumbs to coat our Sweet Chilli Chicken Nuggets (page 96). We often use gluten-free breads as they tend to contain fewer calories and less sugar, so they're an easy swap when you want to shave off a few calories. Panko breadcrumbs make for a time-saving alternative to blitzing your own, and they're available gluten-free! Tortilla wraps are a surprisingly versatile ingredient. Use them as a fibre-loaded way to bundle up your favourite fillings at lunchtime, or let them crisp to perfection in the oven as a lower-calorie 'pastry' alternative. That's one way to get around making pastry from scratch, or you can invest in ready-made puff pastry sheets. It'll save you oodles of time, and it's not too tricky to find lighter, lower-calorie versions.

EGGS

Eggs are protein-rich, tasty and versatile! The humble egg can be used in so many different ways. From baking and binding ingredients together, to having a starring role in our hearty Bobotie (page 178) you'll never go wrong if you have a box of eggs in the house.

LOW-CALORIE COOKING SPRAY

One of the best ways to cut down on cooking with oils and fats is to use a low-calorie cooking spray. A spritz of this will make little difference to the end result of your food, but it can make a huge difference to the number of calories consumed.

SUGAR-FREE HARD BUTTER CANDIES

Using sugar-free hard butter candies is a clever way to add a delectable crunch to our sweet recipes, without the need for lashings of caramel. You'll want them to rustle up our Salted Caramel Froyo recipe (page 222).

SWEETENER

There are so many sweeteners out there, it can be tricky to know which is the best substitute for regular sugar. Sweeteners vary in sweetness and swapping them weight-for-weight with regular sugar can give you different results. In our recipes we use granulated sweetener, not powdered sweetener, as it has larger 'crystals'. This can be used weight-for-weight anywhere you're replacing sugar.

DRIED PASTA *and* NOODLES

We wouldn't want to live without pasta or noodles! They're not too pricey to stock up on, and they'll keep nicely in the store cupboard until you're ready to transform them into midweek classics and fakeaway favourites, like our speedy Peanut Ramen (page 62).

MARMITE

Love it or hate it (sorry, we had to!), there's no denying that Marmite is a budget-friendly way to unlock new levels of savoury flavour. If you don't believe us, ask our Cheesy Marmite Pasta Bake (page 160).

SELF-RAISING FLOUR, BAKING POWDER *and* ROLLED OATS

Whether you're an expert or beginner baker, you'll want to make sure you've got self-raising flour. It's an essential ingredient to guarantee the fluffiness of cakes, muffins and other baked goodies. You'll want to sift your flour together with baking powder, so that your spongy treats will rise in the oven. To make the slimming-friendly topping for our Orange and Ginger Rhubarb Crumble (page 208), we use rolled oats that are rich in fibre. They're always handy to have in the cupboard, and not just for breakfast!

BISCOFF SMOOTH SPREAD

We don't need telling twice to stock up on Biscoff! This is a spreadable version of the biscuit of the same name; it's the smooth variety (not the crunchy one) we use to create all kinds of velvety, caramelised biscuit-flavoured treats.

ESSENTIAL KIT

NON-STICK PANS

If there's one bit of kit that Pinch of Nom would advise as an investment kitchen piece, it would be a decent set of non-stick pans. The better the non-stick quality of your pans, the fewer cooking oils and fats you'll need to use in order to stop food sticking and burning. Keep your pans in good health by cleaning them properly and gently with soapy water. We recommend picking up a good set of saucepans, as well as a small and a large frying pan.

KITCHEN KNIVES *and* KNIFE SHARPENER

Every kitchen needs a good set of knives. If you can, invest in some good-quality, super-sharp knives – blunt knives have a habit of bouncing off ingredients, which can make them more dangerous than sharper ones. You'll need to mind your fingers with super-sharp knives too, but you'll be glad you invested when you've got knives that glide through veg, saving you so much time and effort. Once you've invested in your sharp knives, you'll want to keep them that way! Keep those babies nice and sharp so you can carry on slicing and dicing like a pro.

CHOPPING BOARDS

As well as protecting your surfaces, a good set of chopping boards are the key to a safe and hygienic kitchen. We'd suggest picking up a full set of colour-coordinated chopping boards, with separate boards for veg, meat, fish and dairy. They'll make it so much easier to keep your ingredients separate and most sets are easy to clean and tidy away once your meal prep is sorted.

HOB

We cook on an induction hob. If you have a ceramic/hot-plate hob you may have to cook dishes for a little longer.

OVENWARE

For almost every oven recipe you'll need either an oven tray, roasting tin or oven dish. We'd recommend making sure you've got some baking sheets, square and round cake tins, a loaf tin, a large, heavy-based casserole dish with a lid, a pie dish, quiche dish and lasagne dish as essential items. If a specific size of dish is essential to the success of a recipe, we've listed this as 'Special Equipment'.

BAKING PAPER *and* KITCHEN FOIL

Keep your ovenware in tip-top condition for longer by lining them with non-stick baking paper before cooking. As well as helping to keep your ovenware clean, kitchen foil is handy for preventing food from drying out. Use foil to wrap up or cover meat, fish and vegetables so that it retains moisture in the oven.

SLOW COOKER

We're big fans of slow cookers. Throw in some ingredients, go out, enjoy your day and return to a home-cooked meal, ready and waiting for you. They're a relatively inexpensive bit of kit that will save you a lot of time. We use a 3.5-litre slow cooker – please don't attempt to make our dishes in a slow cooker that is any smaller than this.

ELECTRIC PRESSURE COOKER

A pressure cooker is a great investment if you're looking to save time. The high-pressure cooking process creates perfectly tender meat and makes stews taste as though they've been bubbling away for hours. We recommend electric models for safety and ease of use.

AIR FRYER

Air fryers have become a slimming staple in recent years. They give you crispy, deep-fried textures and flavours without having to plunge your food into high-calorie oils. The ultimate in convenience, food cooks more quickly in an air fryer, and any excess cooking oils drain away for a lighter, crispier finish. They're great for chips, breaded meats and so much more. If your air fryer doesn't have a preheat function, heat it at cooking temperature for a few minutes before air-frying your food.

FOOD PROCESSOR, BLENDER, STICK BLENDER *and* ELECTRIC WHISK

These are essential pieces of kit for a lot of Pinch of Nom recipes. We like to make sauces from scratch, so a decent blender or food processor is a lifesaver. A stick blender can be used on most occasions if you're looking for something cheaper or more compact. It's well worth the investment for the flavour of all those homemade sauces. An electric whisk is nice to have when you need to whip up a scrummy sweet treat in a hurry.

MIXING BOWLS

A couple of mixing bowls will come in handy time and time again. We'd suggest getting at least two, a smaller one and a large one will see you through most kinds of recipes. Smaller bowls give you more control when you're whisking ingredients and larger bowls mean there's more room to mix it up.

MUFFIN TRAY, PASTRY CUTTERS AND A WIRE RACK

From Banana and Blueberry Muffins (page 122) to Egg and Bacon Pies (page 124), a muffin tray makes it simple to prepare sweet and savoury bakes by the batch. Make sure your muffin tray is deep enough to hold a whole egg! All of your baked goodies will cool down quicker on a rack. While it can be tough to resist, resting time is essential to prevent a soggy bottom. Pastry cutters will effortlessly slice your readymade sheets into impressive shapes for minimum effort.

LOOSE-BOTTOMED TART TIN

There's nothing worse than seeing all of your hard work crumble! With a loose-bottomed tin that has a base that easily lifts away, there's no need to turn cakes, tarts, quiches or pies upside down. Phew!

MEASURING SPOONS

Want to make sure you never get muddled between a tsp and tbsp? Pinch of Nom has absolutely, definitely never made this mistake. Honest. But these days we're never without a trusty set of measuring spoons, which help make sure it's not a tablespoon of chilli when it should have been a teaspoon. Just make sure you use a butter knife to level off the spoon – you'll be surprised how much extra you add when the spoonful is heaped.

HEATPROOF JUG

A measuring jug is essential for measuring out wet ingredients. We recommend getting a heatproof version that you can stick in the microwave when needed.

FINE GRATER

Using a fine grater is one of those surprising revelations. You won't believe the difference between grating cheese with a fine grater versus a standard grater. 45g of cheese, for example, can easily cover an oven dish when using a fine grater. You can also use it for citrus zest, garlic and ginger – it helps a little go a long, long way.

POTATO MASHER

Used in a number of recipes, you'll need a decent masher to make sure you've got smooth, creamy mash to spoon onto your dishes, or for making the Mashed Potato Balls on page 112.

GARLIC CRUSHER

You'll never miss the faff of finely chopping garlic once you've invested in a garlic crusher. Relatively cheap to pick up, you won't go back after you've squeezed that first clove into a perfect paste. It'll save you so much time and it helps your garlic spread evenly throughout the dish.

WOODEN *or* METAL SKEWERS

Threading meat, fish or vegetables onto skewers means they'll leave the oven or air fryer with so much more deliciously juicy flavour. You can keep turning them for even cooking, and you can make sure every inch of your meat is covered with marinade. Be sure to soak wooden skewers in water before using them, so that they don't catch and burn.

TUPPERWARE *and* PLASTIC TUBS

Most of the Pinch of Nom recipes in this book are freezable and ideal for batch cooking. It's a good idea to invest in some freezerproof tubs – and they don't have to be plastic. For a more eco-friendly solution, choose glass storage containers; just remember to check they're freezer-safe. And don't forget, it's always a good idea to add a label with what it is, and on what date you put it in the freezer!

*Note on plastic: We have made a conscious effort to reduce the amount of non-reusable plastic, such as cling film, when making our recipes. There are great alternatives to cling film now available, such as silicone stretch lids, beeswax food covers, fabric food covers and biodegradable food and freezer bags.

Quick
COOK

VEGGIE

USE VEGETARIAN MINCE

DAIRY FREE

USE DF CHEESE

GLUTEN FREE

USE GF WRAPS

BREAKFAST TACOS

🕐 **15 MINS**   🍲 **15 MINS**   ✕ **SERVES 4**

PER SERVING:
326 KCAL /27G CARBS

2 medium eggs, beaten
4 small soft low-calorie tortilla wraps or taco wraps, about 18cm / 7in diameter
15g reduced-fat mature Cheddar, finely grated
sea salt and freshly ground black pepper
lime wedges, to serve (optional)

FOR THE AVOCADO SALSA

1 avocado, stoned and mashed
2 spring onions, thinly sliced
5g fresh coriander leaves, finely chopped
8 cherry tomatoes, diced
1 tbsp lime juice
¼ tsp sriracha sauce

FOR THE PORK

low-calorie cooking spray
1 medium red onion, peeled and diced
200g 5%-fat minced pork
½ tsp paprika
¼ tsp chilli powder
¼ tsp garlic granules
¼ tsp onion granules
¼ tsp dried oregano
¼ tsp ground cumin
1 tbsp tomato puree

Step away from the cereal – we've got something far more fun for breakfast! A Mexican-inspired twist on sausage and eggs, our Breakfast Tacos will spice up your morning. These loaded tacos are ready in just 30 minutes, start to finish. Perfect for a weekend brunch, you can even throw on extra toppings like jalapeños, sliced red chilli, or sour cream if you don't mind adding a few extra calories.

Everyday Light ─────────────────────

Start by preparing the pork mixture. Spray a frying pan with low-calorie cooking spray and place over a medium heat. Add the onion and fry for 5 minutes, then add the pork mince and sprinkle over the paprika, chilli, garlic granules, onion granules, oregano and cumin. Fry for 5 minutes, breaking up the mince with a wooden spoon, until browned. Add the tomato puree and stir until coated.

While the pork is cooking, put the avocado, spring onions, coriander, tomatoes, lime juice and sriracha sauce in a small bowl and stir. Season to taste with salt and pepper and leave to one side.

Add the eggs to a small saucepan and season with salt and pepper. Place over a medium heat and stir with a wooden spoon, folding the eggs over from the bottom of the pan until they are softly set. Remove from the heat and leave to one side while you assemble the tacos.

Spread the wraps with the avocado salsa then add some of the pork mince to one half of the taco. Add some of the scrambled eggs and finish with a sprinkling of grated cheese. Fold and serve with lime wedges for squeezing over, if you like!

POACHED EGG WITH CRISPY PARMA HAM

🕐 **2 MINS**　　🍲 **8 MINS**　　✕ **SERVES 1**

PER SERVING:
259 KCAL /15G CARBS

1 medium egg
1 small slice Parma ham
1 small, thin slice wholemeal bread
1 tbsp reduced-fat cream cheese
freshly ground black pepper

TO ACCOMPANY (OPTIONAL)
¼ tin baked beans
　(+ 85 kcal per serving)

Need a breakfast that's ready to eat in under 10 minutes? You'll struggle to find something more delicious than this! Your perfectly poached egg sits on a crunchy slice of toast, spread with cream cheese and topped with a piece of crispy, salty Parma ham. All that slimming-friendly protein is perfect first thing in the morning: it'll keep you going till lunchtime.

Everyday Light ————————————

Place a small saucepan of water over a medium heat and bring to a simmer. Crack the egg into the water gently and immediately reduce the heat – there should only be a few small bubbles in the water. If the water is bubbling too much this may cause the egg to move around and break up. Cook gently for 2–4 minutes, depending on how you like your poached eggs to be cooked.

While the egg is cooking, place a small non-stick frying pan over a medium heat. When the frying pan is hot, add the slice of Parma ham (there's no need to spray the frying pan with low-calorie cooking spray). Fry for 1–2 minutes, until any fat around the ham has dissolved and the ham is crispy. Set aside.

Toast the bread to your liking, place on a plate and spread the cream cheese over.

Use a large, slotted spoon to lift the poached egg out of the saucepan and allow any excess water to drain off.

Place the crispy ham on top of the cream cheese and top with the poached egg. Sprinkle over a little black pepper (you may not need to season with salt as the ham will be salty). Serve at once, alone or with an accompaniment of your choice.

TIPS:

If you prefer, you can use a silicone egg poaching pod to place your egg in during poaching.
You could use a bacon medallion or a small slice of lean ham instead of Parma ham and adjust the calories accordingly.

QUICK COOK

VEGGIE

USE VEGETARIAN
ITALIAN HARD
CHEESE AND
OMIT THE HAM

GLUTEN
FREE

USE GF BREAD

GREEN EGGS AND HAM

🕐 **10 MINS** 🍲 **10 MINS** ✕ **SERVES 1**

PER SERVING:
396 KCAL / 20G CARBS

1 slice of Parma ham, any fat
  left on
low-calorie cooking spray
30g frozen garden peas
2 spring onions, trimmed and
  finely chopped
40g baby spinach
2 medium eggs
10g Parmesan, finely grated
a good pinch of garlic powder
1 medium slice of wholemeal
  bread
5g reduced-fat spread, for
  spreading
sea salt and freshly ground
  black pepper

You might have heard this recipe name before: we've taken inspiration from the much-loved children's book! We've mixed lots of vibrant green veg into our softly scrambled eggs. Crisp Parma ham is crumbled over the 'green' eggs and toast for a quick, slimming-friendly breakfast.

Everyday Light ────────────────────

Place a small non-stick frying pan over a medium-high heat. When the frying pan is hot, add the Parma ham slice to the dry pan. There's no need to use low-calorie spray as the ham will fry in the small amount of fat around its edges as the fat melts. Fry for about 1 minute, turning it several times, until dry, crisp and all the fat has disappeared. Place on a plate lined with kitchen towel and set aside.

Lower the heat and spray the frying pan with low-calorie cooking spray. You don't need to wash the frying pan first, but scrape any bits off and mix them in with the low-calorie spray. Add the frozen peas and spring onions and stir-fry for about 2 minutes, until the peas have defrosted and the spring onion has softened. Add the spinach leaves and stir-fry for a further minute, until just wilted and still bright green. Remove the frying pan from the heat and set aside.

Crack the eggs into a small bowl and beat with a fork until broken up and evenly mixed. Add the Parmesan, garlic powder and 2 tablespoons of cold water and stir. Season well with salt and pepper.

Toast the bread to your liking. Spread the reduced-fat spread over the toast and place on a plate.

While the bread is toasting, place the frying pan containing the vegetables over a medium heat. When the pan is hot, pour in the egg mixture and move it gently around the pan using a spatula, incorporating the vegetables. Cook gently for 2–3 minutes, until still a little runny around the edges, then remove from the heat. The residual heat in the frying pan will finish cooking the egg until it's softly scrambled.

Place the scrambled egg and green vegetable mixture on top of the toast. Break up the crisp Parma ham and sprinkle over the top. Serve at once.

TIP:

You could use bacon medallions or cooked ham instead of Parma ham. Cooked ham can be chopped and added to the finished dish. Remember to adjust the calories accordingly.

QUICK COOK

26

VEGGIE

USE 'VEGGIE' BACON AND CHORIZO

FREEZE ME

PANCAKES ONLY

DAIRY FREE

USE DF MILK, CHEESE AND YOGHURT

SAVOURY BREAKFAST PANCAKES

🕐 **15 MINS**　🍲 **15 MINS**　✕ **SERVES 2**

PER SERVING:
396 KCAL / 43G CARBS

10g chorizo, diced
1 bacon medallion, cut into strips

FOR THE PANCAKES
100g self-raising flour
2 medium eggs, beaten
100ml skimmed milk
¼ tsp garlic granules
5g reduced-fat mature Cheddar,
　finely grated
3g chives, finely chopped
low-calorie cooking spray
sea salt and freshly ground
　black pepper

FOR THE SALSA
2 cherry tomatoes, diced
1 spring onion, thinly sliced
¼ red chilli, deseeded and finely
　diced
4g fresh coriander leaves, finely
　chopped
¼ avocado, peeled, stoned and
　mashed
½ tsp sriracha sauce
2 tbsp fat-free Greek yoghurt
¼ tsp reduced-sugar ketchup

TO ACCOMPANY (OPTIONAL)
1 medium fried egg
　(+ 82 kcal per serving)

Flavoured with cheese and chives, these pancakes will be your new favourite way to start the day. Our cross between a salsa and guacamole makes for a delicious savoury topping, with fresh tomatoes, avocado and a hint of chilli. Drizzle over the creamy yoghurt mixture and add a lovely saltiness by sprinkling on some crispy bacon and chorizo.

Everyday Light ───────────────────────

First, make the pancake batter. Add the flour, eggs and milk to a bowl and whisk together until fully combined. Add the garlic granules, Cheddar and chives, season with salt and pepper and whisk again. Leave to rest for 5 minutes.

While the pancake batter is resting, prepare the salsa. Put the tomatoes, spring onion, red chilli, coriander, avocado and ¼ teaspoon of the sriracha sauce in a small bowl and mix well. Set aside.

Add the chorizo and bacon to a small frying pan and cook over a low heat for 2–3 minutes until crispy. Set aside.

Once the batter has rested, spray a clean frying pan with low-calorie cooking spray and place over a medium heat. When the pan is hot, spoon in some of the mixture and spread into a small pancake shape. Don't spread it too far as you want a fluffy pancake. You can cook several at once, depending on the size of your pan. Cook for 2–3 minutes, until bubbles appear on the surface and it's lightly golden underneath. Flip over and cook for a few more minutes. Stack on a plate and cover with kitchen foil to keep them warm.

Repeat until all the batter is used. We made 6 pancakes with our mixture, but it depends how small or large you spread the batter. The pancakes can be frozen at this point, layered between sheets of non-stick baking paper and placed in a freezerproof container. Follow standard guidelines for defrosting and reheating.

Add the yoghurt, ketchup and remaining ¼ teaspoon of sriracha to a small bowl and mix. Stack up the pancakes on 2 serving plates, add a spoonful of the salsa, spoon over the crispy chorizo and bacon and finish with a dollop of the yoghurt mixture.

TERIYAKI CHICKEN DONBURI

🕐 **15 MINS** 🍲 **20 MINS** ✕ **SERVES 4**

* PLUS 1 HOUR MARINATING

PER SERVING:
368 KCAL /51G CARBS

500g skinless and boneless chicken thighs (visible fat removed)
200g basmati rice
2 carrots, peeled and cut into matchsticks
60g pea shoots
2 spring onions, trimmed and thinly sliced
lime wedges, to serve (optional)

FOR THE CHICKEN MARINADE
2 tbsp dark soy sauce
2 tbsp white granulated sweetener
1 tbsp rice wine vinegar
1 tbsp fish sauce
1 tbsp honey
1 tbsp tomato puree
1 garlic clove, peeled and crushed
¼ tsp ground ginger
¼ tsp dried chilli flakes
juice of 1 lime

Save a few pennies and make this restaurant favourite in the comfort of your own kitchen. Donburi is a traditional Japanese dish where meat or fish is served over a bed of rice. In our version, we've swapped sushi rice for basmati to make it more store-cupboard friendly, and it's just as tasty! Once your chicken has had time to marinate, this recipe comes together really quickly. Fluffy rice, tender chicken thighs and crunchy veggies . . . what more could you ask for?

Everyday Light ————————————

Put all the chicken marinade ingredients in a bowl and stir well. Add the chicken thighs and coat in the marinade, cover and place in the fridge for a minimum of 1 hour to allow the flavours to develop.

Preheat the oven to 210°C (fan 190°C /gas mark 6).

Remove the chicken thighs from the marinade and place onto a baking tray, discarding any leftover marinade. Bake the chicken in the oven for 20 minutes or until cooked through: they should show no signs of pinkness and the juices should run clear.

While the chicken is cooking, rinse the rice in a colander until the water runs clear. Shake it to remove the excess water, then cook the rice according to the packet instructions (this should take about 10 minutes). For fluffier rice, once the rice is tender, turn off the heat and leave covered with the lid. This will absorb any extra water from the pan and give you really fluffy rice!

Once the chicken thighs are cooked through, slice them up. Add a spoonful of cooked rice to the bottom of a bowl, top with the sliced chicken, carrot and a handful of pea shoots, sprinkle with the spring onion and serve with lime wedges on the side if you like!

TIP:
You can slice the carrots into matchsticks, grate them or use a julienne peeler.

FAKEAWAYS

FREEZE ME

PATTIES ONLY

DAIRY FREE

USE DF CHEESE SLICES AND MAYONNAISE

GLUTEN FREE

USE GF BURGER BUNS, SOY SAUCE AND BREADCRUMBS

BEEF AND PINEAPPLE BURGERS

🕐 **15 MINS**   🍲 **15 MINS**   ✕ **SERVES 4**

PER SERVING:
335 KCAL /33G CARBS

SPECIAL EQUIPMENT
Small frying pan

FOR THE BURGER PATTIES
250g 5%-fat minced beef
20g panko breadcrumbs
¼ tsp garlic granules
¼ tsp onion granules
¼ tsp mustard powder
¼ tsp smoked sweet paprika
¼ tsp BBQ seasoning
low-calorie cooking spray

FOR THE PINEAPPLE SALSA
100g fresh peeled, cored
   pineapple, finely diced
80g deseeded green pepper,
   finely diced
1 tsp sweet chilli sauce
½ tsp lime juice
½ tsp soy sauce

FOR THE SWEET CHILLI MAYO
2 tbsp reduced-fat mayonnaise
1 tbsp sweet chilli sauce
1 tsp lime juice
¼ tsp sriracha sauce

TO ASSEMBLE
4 seeded burger buns (about
   40g each), sliced in half
50g lettuce leaves
2 reduced-fat Cheddar slices,
   halved
1 tomato, sliced

If you've never tried beef with pineapple before, this is the place to start. Using a few nifty lower-calorie swaps, we've brought these juicy, cheese-topped burgers down to just 315 calories each – chilli mayo, fruity salsa and seeded burger buns included! Do your next fakeaway night right by piling them high with our slimming-friendly salsa.

Everyday Light ─────────────────

To make the burger patties, put the beef mince, panko breadcrumbs, garlic granules, onion granules, mustard powder, paprika and BBQ seasoning in a mixing bowl and mix with clean hands until well combined.

Divide into 4 equal portions and shape into 4 burger patties. Set aside. At this point, the patties can be frozen if you wish (or they can be frozen once cooked). Wrap each patty individually, then place in a freezerproof container. Defrost overnight in the fridge before reheating cooked patties in the microwave until piping hot or cooking raw patties in a frying pan.

To make the pineapple salsa, spray a small frying pan with low-calorie cooking spray and place over a medium heat. Add the pineapple and green pepper and fry for 4 minutes until softened slightly, then add the sweet chilli sauce, lime juice and soy sauce. Stir to combine and set aside.

Spray a clean frying pan with low-calorie cooking spray and place over a medium heat. Add the burger patties and fry for 4–5 minutes on each side or until cooked through.

While the burger patties are cooking, make the sweet chilli mayo. In a small bowl, mix the mayonnaise, sweet chilli sauce, lime juice and sriracha sauce until combined.

Once the burgers are cooked, turn off the heat. Add half a cheese slice to the top of each one and leave to melt.

Toast the inside of the burger buns. Spread the bottom half of each bun with a little of the sweet chilli mayo. Add some lettuce leaves, a burger patty with cheese on, some sliced tomato then pile on the pineapple salsa. Finish with a little more of the sweet chilli mayo and serve.

SZECHUAN-STYLE NOODLES

🕐 **15 MINS**　　🍲 **15 MINS**　　✕ **SERVES 4**

PER SERVING:
403 KCAL /47G CARBS

2 tsp Szechuan peppercorns

4 tsp tahini paste or peanut butter

6 tbsp soy sauce

4 tsp rice vinegar

1 tsp white granulated sweetener or sugar

low-calorie cooking spray

400g 2%-fat minced turkey

2.5cm (1in) piece of root ginger, peeled and finely grated

2 garlic cloves, peeled and crushed

½ tsp Chinese 5 spice

4 tbsp oyster sauce

1 chicken stock pot

4 x 50g nests of dried egg noodles

100g pak choi, trimmed and cut into bite-sized chunks

1 x 410g tin beansprouts in water, drained

TO SERVE
handful of fresh coriander leaves, chopped

2 red chillies (seeds in), thinly sliced into rings

Sometimes called dan dan noodles, this speedy stir-fry is inspired by a Chinese street food dish that is usually served with lashings of chilli oil. We've replaced the oil with a sprinkling of fresh sliced chillies. Szechuan peppercorns have a unique, slightly citrusy taste, adding aromatic flavour and another level of heat to this fiery recipe.

Weekly Indulgence

Prepare the Szechuan peppercorns: pick out and discard any hard black seeds, then place the peppercorns in a dry frying pan and toast over a medium heat for about 6 minutes or until they become fragrant and start to crackle. This will release their flavour. Allow to cool, then grind to a powder using a pestle and mortar or spice grinder.

Place the ground Szechuan pepper in a small mixing bowl with the tahini paste, soy sauce, rice vinegar and sweetener or sugar and stir until well combined. Set aside.

Spray a wok or large frying pan with low-calorie cooking spray and place over a high heat. Add the turkey mince and stir-fry for 5 minutes, until thoroughly cooked. Add the ginger, garlic and Chinese 5 spice and cook for a further minute. Stir in the oyster sauce and continue to fry for a minute or two until the turkey is well coated, then transfer to a bowl and keep warm.

Bring a large saucepan of water to the boil, add the chicken stock pot and stir until dissolved. Add the noodles and cook for 4 minutes.

While the noodles are cooking, pour the Szechuan sauce mixture into the wok or frying pan (no need to wash it first), and heat until bubbling. Add the pak choi and beansprouts.

When the noodles are cooked, drain, reserving a little of the cooking liquid. Stir the noodles into the sauce and coat thoroughly. Add a few spoonfuls of the reserved cooking liquid if they are too dry.

Divide the noodles between bowls and top with the turkey mixture. Sprinkle over the chopped coriander leaves and sliced red chillies, to taste.

TIP:
We've left the seeds in our sliced red chillies to give a fiery heat, but if you prefer less heat you can remove the seeds.

VEGGIE

SWAP CHICKEN
FOR QUORN

FREEZE
ME

BATCH
COOK

DAIRY
FREE

GLUTEN
FREE

USE GF SOY
SAUCE

CASHEW NUT CHICKEN

🕐 **15 MINS**   🍲 **15 MINS**   ✕ **SERVES 4**

PER SERVING:
274 KCAL / 19G CARBS

3 tbsp light soy sauce
2 tbsp mirin
1 tsp honey
½ tsp ground ginger
½ tsp sriracha sauce
1 tbsp cornflour
low-calorie cooking spray
1 onion, peeled and cut into
    chunks
3 garlic cloves, peeled and
    crushed
80g button mushrooms,
    quartered
2 medium skinless chicken
    breasts (visible fat removed),
    about 260g in total, cut into
    thin strips
80g broccoli, cut into small
    florets
80g cashew nuts

TO ACCOMPANY
50g uncooked basmati rice per
    portion, cooked according to
    packet instructions (+ 173 kcal
    per 125g cooked serving)

Put down the takeaway menu! There's no need to order when you can rustle up our Cashew Nut Chicken from the comfort of your own kitchen. We've raided our store cupboard for the ingredients to make our mildly-spiced sauce, and stir-fried it together with chicken pieces, chopped veg and crunchy cashew nuts. Ready in just 30 minutes, it's a surefire weekend winner with rice or noodles!

Everyday Light

Combine the soy sauce, mirin, honey, ginger, sriracha, cornflour and 4 tablespoons of water in a small bowl. Stir until smooth and set aside.

Spray a large frying pan or wok with low-calorie cooking spray and place over a medium heat. Add the onion, garlic and mushrooms and fry for 5 minutes, until the onion has softened slightly and the mushrooms have coloured. Add the chicken strips and stir-fry for 3–4 minutes or until golden brown on all sides.

Add the broccoli and pour in the soy sauce mixture. Simmer for 3 minutes until the chicken is coated and the broccoli is tender (but still retains a little crispness), and the sauce has reduced.

Stir in the cashew nuts and serve with your choice of accompaniment. We think this is great with basmati rice.

The chicken will keep in the fridge for up to 3 days. To freeze, follow standard guidelines for defrosting and reheating.

TIP:
If you can't find mirin, you can substitute with rice wine or dry sherry instead.

CHILLI CRAB LINGUINE

🕐 **10 MINS**　　🍲 **15 MINS**　　✕ **SERVES 4**

PER SERVING:
371 KCAL / 58G CARBS

300g dried linguine
low-calorie cooking spray
½ medium red onion, peeled and
　finely chopped
2 garlic cloves, peeled and finely
　chopped
1 red chilli, seeds left in and
　finely chopped
80g frozen peas
200g cherry tomatoes, halved
2 x 170g tins white shredded
　crabmeat in brine, drained
150ml fish or chicken stock
　(½ fish or chicken stock cube
　dissolved in 150ml boiling
　water)
50g reduced-fat cream cheese
10g flat-leaf parsley leaves,
　roughly chopped
sea salt and freshly ground
　black pepper

Need a quick, tasty dinner that'll impress your friends and family? This speedy pasta dish brings so much flavour to the table, no one will guess how easy it is to make. It turns tinned white crabmeat into a dinner that tastes just as good as restaurant versions, for a fraction of the calories. We'd say this recipe is medium hot, thanks to leaving the seeds in our red chilli, but you can add more or less to make it right for you.

Everyday Light ─────────────────────

Cook the linguine in a large saucepan of boiling water for 8–10 minutes, or according to the packet instructions, until tender but it still retains some bite. Drain well, return to the saucepan, cover and set aside.

While the linguine is cooking, spray a large frying pan with low-calorie cooking spray and place over a medium heat. Add the onion and fry for 5 minutes until softened and translucent, then add the garlic and chilli and fry for 1–2 minutes, stirring. Stir in the frozen peas and tomatoes and cook for 2–3 minutes, until the peas are tender and the tomatoes are softening around the edges. Stir in the crabmeat and stock and simmer, uncovered, over a low heat for about 2 minutes to heat through thoroughly.

Add the cream cheese and stir until completely blended in. Tip the crabmeat mixture into the saucepan containing the linguine. Add the parsley and stir until the linguine is lightly coated. Season to taste with salt and pepper, if needed. Serve at once.

TIP:
You can use dried spaghetti or other pasta of your choice instead of linguine, if you prefer.

GREEN VEG PASTA

🕐 **10 MINS**   🍲 **10 MINS**   ✕ **SERVES 4**

VEGGIE

VEGAN
USE DF CHEESE

FREEZE ME

BATCH COOK

GLUTEN FREE
USE GF PASTA

PER SERVING:
281 KCAL / 40G CARBS

200g small dried pasta shapes (any shape you prefer)
low-calorie cooking spray
1 medium leek, trimmed and thinly sliced
2 garlic cloves, peeled and crushed
100g broccoli, cut into bite-sized florets
40g baby spinach leaves
80g frozen peas
3 tbsp low-fat cream cheese
60ml boiling water
40g reduced-fat mature Cheddar, finely grated
sea salt and freshly ground black pepper

This bright-coloured pasta is the definition of quick and easy! Brimming with flavour, you can always trust this lean, green dish to leave you full and satisfied. The pasta sauce alone gets you well on your way to 5-a-day, made with a silky-smooth blend of peas, leek, broccoli, spinach and reduced-fat cream cheese. You can make it gluten-free or vegan with a handful of simple swaps!

Everyday Light ─────────────────────

Cook the pasta in a saucepan of salted boiling water according to the packet instructions – this is usually 8–10 minutes. Drain well, cover and set aside.

While the pasta is cooking, spray a large frying pan with low-calorie cooking spray and place over a medium heat. Add the leek and garlic and fry for 2 minutes, then add the broccoli and fry for a further 4 minutes until starting to soften. Add the spinach leaves and frozen peas and cook for another 4 minutes until the vegetables are soft.

Remove half of the vegetables and add to a food processor with the cream cheese and boiling water. Blitz until smooth. If you don't have a food processor, you can use a stick blender. Pop half of the cooked vegetables into a bowl and blitz until smooth.

Return to the frying pan along with the drained pasta. Stir to coat. Add the Cheddar and stir until combined. Season with salt and pepper and serve.

The dish will keep in the fridge for 1–2 days. To freeze, follow standard guidelines for defrosting and reheating. You may need to add a splash of water before reheating.

FAKEAWAYS

MEATBALLS WITH GINGER AND SPRING ONION

🕐 **15 MINS**   🍲 **20 MINS**   ✕ **SERVES 4**

PER SERVING:
303 KCAL / 24G CARBS

low-calorie cooking spray
1 spring onion, trimmed and cut into fine shreds, to garnish (optional)

FOR THE MEATBALLS
500g 5%-fat minced pork
1 tsp garlic granules
1 tsp onion granules
small pinch of Chinese 5 spice
½ tsp ground ginger
¼ tsp salt
¼ tsp ground black pepper
1 medium egg, beaten

FOR THE SAUCE
1 medium onion, peeled and finely chopped
3cm (1¼in) piece of root ginger, peeled and finely grated
2 tsp garlic granules
6 spring onions, trimmed and thinly sliced
4 tbsp oyster sauce
4 tbsp dark soy sauce
100ml Chinese rice wine
2 tsp white granulated sweetener or sugar
¼ tsp salt

TO ACCOMPANY
50g uncooked basmati rice per portion, cooked according to packet instructions (+ 173 kcal per 125g cooked serving)
(OPTIONAL)
80g steamed vegetables (+ 38 kcal per serving)

You'd never know that these Meatballs with Ginger and Spring Onion aren't from the local Chinese takeaway! We've used slimming-friendly swaps to make sure they're coated in an umami, rich, ginger and spring onion sauce, for just over 300 calories per serving! They'll make for a fantastic fakeaway night feast with a side of rice.

Weekly Indulgence ──────────────

Preheat the oven to 200°C (fan 180°C /gas mark 6) and spray a baking tray with low-calorie cooking spray.

Place the minced pork in a medium mixing bowl and break it up with a wooden spoon. Add all the remaining meatball ingredients except the egg and mix well. Add the beaten egg a little at a time, mixing until you have a mixture that will hold together to make firm meatballs. Shape into 20 small, evenly-sized meatballs. Place the meatballs on the greased baking tray and place in the preheated oven for 15 minutes, until lightly browned.

Now make the sauce. Spray a medium frying pan with low-calorie cooking spray and place over a medium heat. Add the onion and cook for 5–10 minutes, until soft and golden, then reduce the heat and add the root ginger, garlic granules and spring onions. Stir-fry for 2 minutes. Add the oyster sauce, soy sauce, Chinese rice wine, 100ml cold water, sweetener or sugar and salt and stir. Add the cooked meatballs to the sauce and simmer, uncovered, over a low heat for 5 minutes, turning the meatballs to coat them, until the meatballs are piping hot and the sauce has slightly thickened. Serve with rice and some steamed green vegetables, if you wish.

The meatballs and sauce will keep in the fridge for up to 3 days. To freeze, follow standard guidelines for defrosting and reheating.

GARLICKY SURF AND TURF

🕐 **5 MINS**   🍲 **15 MINS**   ✗ **SERVES 4**

*** PLUS 15 MINS FOR STEAKS TO COME TO ROOM TEMPERATURE
AND 5 MINS RESTING AFTER COOKING**

PER SERVING:
341 KCAL / 1.9G CARBS

4 x 227g steaks (rump, sirloin,
   rib eye or fillet, all visible fat
   removed)
low-calorie cooking spray
1 shallot, peeled and finely
   chopped
4 garlic cloves, peeled and
   crushed
250ml beef stock (1 beef stock
   cube dissolved in 250ml boiling
   water)
2 tsp lemon juice
1 tsp white wine vinegar
75g reduced-fat cream cheese
150g cooked, peeled king
   prawns
1 tbsp chopped flat-leaf parsley
   leaves
sea salt and freshly ground
   black pepper
lemon wedges, to serve

TO ACCOMPANY
80g steamed vegetables
   (+ 38 kcal per serving)

Back in the 80s, surf and turf used to mean topping a steak with deep-fried breaded scampi. We've worked some Pinch of Nom magic to bring you this lighter take on the meat and seafood combo! Cook the succulent steak to your liking, then smother it in our slimming-friendly creamy, garlicky sauce, complete with juicy king prawns. Ready in 20 minutes, we love to serve it with steamed green vegetables on the side.

Everyday Light ─────────────────────────

Steaks are always best cooked from room temperature, so take them out of the fridge 15 minutes before cooking. Spray the steaks lightly on both sides with low-calorie cooking spray and season with salt and pepper.

Spray a large frying pan with low-calorie cooking spray and place over a medium-high heat. Add the shallot and sauté for 2–3 minutes, until soft but not coloured. Remove from the pan and set to one side.

Return the pan to the heat and place the steaks in the hot pan. Cook to your liking: the time will vary depending on your preference and how thick your steaks are, but a good guide is 2 minutes each side for rare, 3 each side for medium and 4 each side for well done. A rare steak should feel spongy when pressed, medium will have a little resistance and well done will feel quite firm. Remove the steaks from the pan, place on a plate, cover with foil and allow to rest.

While the steaks rest, cook your sauce. Turn the heat down to medium and return the shallot to the pan, along with the garlic. Cook for 1 minute, then pour in the stock, lemon juice and white wine vinegar. Bring to the boil, then reduce the heat and stir in the cream cheese until evenly blended. If the sauce is a little thin for your liking, simmer (uncovered) for a little longer to reduce and thicken. If the sauce is too thick for your liking, add a little water to thin it. Add the prawns and simmer for 5 minutes, until thoroughly heated through. Stir in the parsley and season the sauce with salt and pepper if you wish.

Serve the steaks with the creamy prawn sauce and a wedge of lemon.

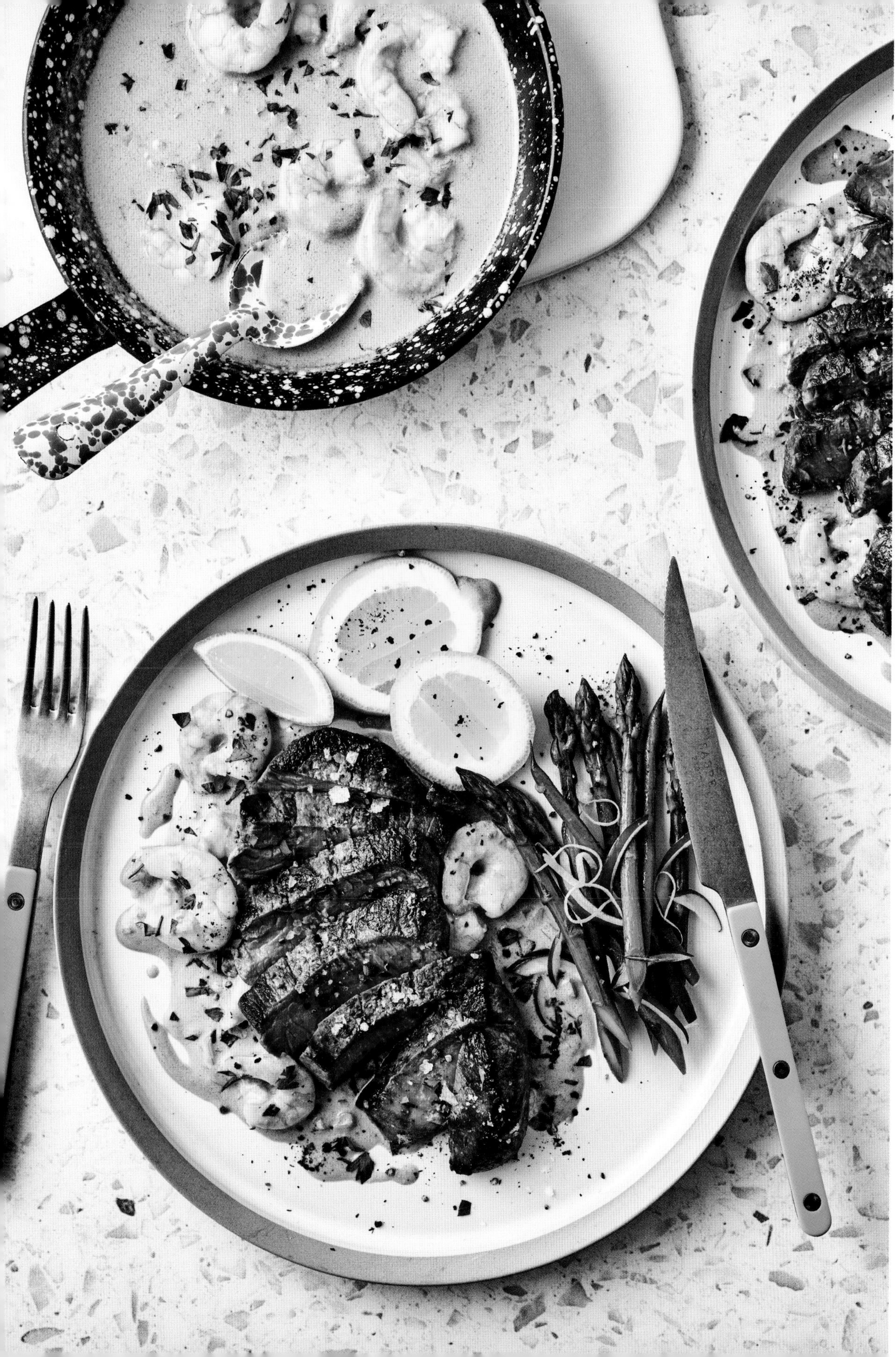

TAMARIND CHICKEN

🕐 **10 MINS**   🍲 **25 MINS**   ✕ **SERVES 4**

PER SERVING:
279 KCAL /13G CARBS

low-calorie cooking spray
500g diced chicken breast
1 medium onion, peeled and
  sliced
1 medium pepper (any colour),
  deseeded and sliced
3cm (1¼in) piece of root ginger,
  peeled and finely grated
3 garlic cloves, peeled and
  crushed
2 tbsp tamarind paste
1 x 400ml tin light coconut milk
2 tbsp light soy sauce
1 chicken stock cube, crumbled
100g green beans, halved
100g sugar snap peas, halved
handful of fresh coriander
  leaves, chopped

TO ACCOMPANY
50g uncooked basmati rice per
  portion, cooked according to
  packet instructions (+ 173 kcal
  per 125g cooked serving)

If you love Thai-style food, this one's for you! Bringing the fragrant flavours without the fiery spices, we've used tamarind paste to add a tasty hint of tanginess to this easy, creamy dish. Sour and slightly tart, tamarind tastes a bit like citrus fruit, similar to limes. It blends beautifully with the creaminess of light coconut milk to create a slimming-friendly sauce to pair with the tender chicken and vegetables in this recipe.

Weekly Indulgence

Spray a large saucepan or wok with low-calorie cooking spray and place over a medium heat. Add the chicken, onion and pepper and sauté for 5 minutes until the chicken is sealed and the vegetables have softened, then add the ginger and garlic and cook for 1 minute.

Stir in the tamarind paste then add the coconut milk, soy sauce and crumbled stock cube (no need to make this up with water). Bring to a simmer and cook for 10 minutes, then add the beans and sugar snap peas and cook for a further 5 minutes.

Stir in the coriander and serve with rice.

The chicken will keep in the fridge for up to 3 days. To freeze, follow standard guidelines for defrosting and reheating.

BEEF WITH CHILLI AND GARLIC

🕐 **10 MINS** 🍲 **10 MINS** ✕ **SERVES 2**

PER SERVING:
284 KCAL / 10G CARBS

350g lean beef strips, suitable for stir-frying, e.g., rump steak, cut into thin strips or beef stir-fry strips

½ tsp Chinese 5-spice

low-calorie cooking spray

½ red pepper, deseeded and sliced

½ green pepper, deseeded and sliced

1 red chilli, deseeded and finely sliced

3 garlic cloves, peeled and crushed

2 tbsp dark soy sauce

1 tbsp rice vinegar

1 tsp white granulated sweetener

½ tsp ground ginger

½ tsp chilli powder

2 spring onions, trimmed and thinly sliced

TO ACCOMPANY

50g uncooked basmati rice per portion, cooked according to packet instructions (+ 173 kcal per 125g cooked serving) or 50g nest of egg noodles per portion, cooked according to packet instructions (+ 171 kcal per serving)

Looking for a tasty fakeaway that's ready in a flash? You can have this speedy stir-fry plated up in 20 minutes, and you'll be impressed with how much flavour you can create in so little time. Using lean beef helps to keep this recipe nice and slimming friendly, so you can serve it with a side of basmati rice, noodles or your favourite Chinese-inspired side dishes from our website.

Weekly Indulgence ———————————

Put the beef strips on a plate and sprinkle over the Chinese 5-spice. Toss to coat.

Spray a large frying pan or wok with low-calorie cooking spray and place over a medium heat. Add the beef strips and fry for 4–5 minutes until browned on all sides. Transfer the beef strips to a plate and leave to one side.

Add the red pepper, green pepper, chilli and garlic to the pan and fry for 2 minutes.

Combine the soy sauce, rice vinegar, sweetener, ginger and chilli powder in a small bowl, pour into the pan and stir to coat the vegetables for 1 minute. Add the beef strips back to the pan and cook for a minute until heated through.

Sprinkle with sliced spring onions and serve with basmati rice or egg noodles (note that these are not gluten free).

The beef will keep in the fridge for up to 3 days. To freeze, follow standard guidelines for defrosting and reheating.

QUICK COOK

BOURBON GLAZED CHICKEN

🕐 **10 MINS**   🍲 **12 MINS**   ✕ **SERVES 4**

FREEZE ME

BATCH COOK

DAIRY FREE

GLUTEN FREE

USE GF SOY SAUCE

PER SERVING:
236 KCAL / 12G CARBS

low-calorie cooking spray
560g chicken breast, cut into strips
sea salt and freshly ground black pepper
2 spring onions, trimmed and thinly sliced, to serve

FOR THE GLAZE
2 garlic cloves, peeled and crushed
2cm (¾in) piece of root ginger, peeled and grated
30ml dark soy sauce
½ tbsp rice vinegar
½ tsp dried chilli flakes
1 tbsp tomato ketchup
60ml bourbon (or other whisky)
2 tbsp runny honey

TO ACCOMPANY
50g uncooked basmati rice per portion, cooked according to packet instructions (+ 173 kcal per 125g cooked serving)

This no-fuss Bourbon Glazed Chicken recipe is pure sweet and sticky comfort food. A speedy answer to 'what do you fancy for dinner tonight?', you can't say no to chicken strips coated in a moreish Asian-inspired glaze. We've used simple store-cupboard staples to get the fakeaway flavours just right. Bourbon enriches our sauce with its signature subtle smokiness (use orange juice to rustle up a non-boozy version).

Weekly Indulgence

Put the glaze ingredients in a bowl, mix well and set aside.

Spray a large wok or frying pan with low-calorie cooking spray and place over a medium heat. Add the chicken and fry for 7–8 minutes, until golden brown and cooked through. You can do this in two batches, if you need to (to avoid overcrowding the pan). Remove the chicken from the pan and set aside.

Wipe out the wok or pan with some kitchen towel and add the glaze to the pan. Turn up the heat and let it bubble rapidly for about 2 minutes, until the liquid has reduced by half. The sauce should be thick and glossy.

Return the chicken to the pan, turn the heat down low and cook for a minute or two, stirring well, to ensure the chicken is piping hot and well coated in the sauce.

Taste, season with salt and pepper if required, and serve sprinkled with the sliced spring onions and rice.

TIP:
Make your chicken spicier by adding extra chilli flakes!

FAKEAWAYS

HAM, CHEESE AND SPINACH OMELETTE WRAP

⏱ **10 MINS**   🍲 **3 MINS**   ✕ **SERVES 2**

PER SERVING:
368 KCAL /25G CARBS

4 medium eggs
low-calorie cooking spray
2 small soft tortilla wraps (about 18cm/7in diameter)
sea salt and freshly ground black pepper

FOR THE FILLING
50g reduced-fat cream cheese
20g Parmesan, finely grated
2 thin slices of cooked ham (about 40g in total), cut into small squares
40g baby spinach leaves
small pinch of fine garlic granules, to taste

Can't choose between a wrap and an omelette for lunch? Put them both together and you get this Ham, Cheese and Spinach Omelette Wrap that you can enjoy hot or cold. The double layer of tortilla wrap and thin, silky omelette is perfect for wrapping up all kinds of fillings. Start with this classic cheese, ham and spinach combination and get more creative each time you make it!

Everyday Light

Crack the eggs into a small bowl and beat with a fork until broken up and evenly mixed. Season with salt and pepper.

Spray a small non-stick frying pan with low-calorie cooking spray and place over a low-medium heat. When the pan is hot, add half of the eggs and tilt the pan slightly so that the eggs swirl around to completely cover the bottom of the pan.

Cook gently for 1–2 minutes, without stirring, until the eggs have set like a very thin omelette and are nearly cooked, but are still wet on the surface. While the egg mixture is still wet on the surface, place a tortilla wrap on top. Press the wrap down lightly with a fish slice so that it sticks to the egg.

Flip the egg and wrap over using a fish slice, so that the egg is facing up. Cook the underside for about 30 seconds, or until the tortilla wrap is lightly golden. Slide the omelette wrap onto a plate, with the egg side facing up.

Spread half of the cream cheese along the centre of the omelette wrap and sprinkle over half of the Parmesan. Scatter over half of the ham and spinach and season to taste with a small pinch of fine garlic granules, salt and pepper. Fold the sides into the centre to encase the filling. Repeat to make a second omelette wrap, and serve warm or cold, alone or with a crisp mixed salad, tomato ketchup or other accompaniment of your choice.

TIPS:
You can use cooked chicken, bacon or other cold cooked meat or cooked fish of your own choice if you prefer. You can substitute the spinach leaves with any other salad leaves of your choice.

VEGGIE

USE QUORN CHUNKS OR CHICKEN SUBSTITUTE AND VEGETABLE STOCK CUBES

VEGAN

USE PLANT-BASED CHICKEN SUBSTITUTE AND VEGAN STOCK

FREEZE ME

BATCH COOK

DAIRY FREE

GLUTEN FREE

USE GF STOCK CUBES

YELLOW THAI-STYLE CURRY

🕐 **30 MINS**　　🍲 **20 MINS**　　✕ **SERVES 4**

PER SERVING:
311 KCAL / 21G CARBS

FOR THE CURRY PASTE
1 dried lemongrass stalk
1 red chilli, deseeded (or leave the seeds in for extra heat)
4 garlic cloves, peeled
5cm (2in) piece of root ginger, peeled
1 onion, peeled and quartered
2 tsp ground coriander
2 tsp ground turmeric

FOR THE CURRY
low-calorie cooking spray
600g diced chicken breast
400ml plant-based coconut drink
2 red, orange or yellow peppers, deseeded and thinly sliced
2 carrots, peeled and thinly sliced into strips
2 chicken stock cubes
2 tbsp peanut butter powder
sea salt and freshly ground black pepper
1 tbsp cornflour, mixed to a slurry with 1 tbsp water (optional)

TO ACCOMPANY
50g uncooked basmati rice per portion, cooked according to packet instructions (+ 173 kcal per 125g cooked serving)

TIP:
You can make the paste in advance and store in an airtight container in the fridge for up to a week or the freezer for up to 3 months.

If you're always drawn to the peanut satay option on restaurant menus, you'll adore this aromatic dish. A tasty alternative to green Thai-inspired curries, our yellow sauce comes jam-packed with moreish, peanutty goodness by adding low-calorie peanut butter powder. Once you've plated up your bright and colourful servings, everyone around the table will feel like they've ordered from a takeaway!

Weekly Indulgence ─────────────

Put all the paste ingredients into a food processor or blender and blitz to a thick paste, pushing the mixture down from the edges of the processor or blender bowl with a spatula from time to time. Transfer to a glass bowl or jar, cover tightly (otherwise it will taint everything in the fridge) and refrigerate.

Spray a frying pan or wok with low-calorie cooking spray and place over a medium heat. When hot and sizzling, add the chicken and let it colour on all sides for 2–3 minutes. Remove the cooked chicken chunks from the pan, then put the curry paste in the pan and fry it for a minute. Pour in the coconut drink and add the rest of the curry ingredients (except the chicken), crumbling in the stock cubes. Stir, bring to the boil, then reduce the heat and simmer for 10 minutes, stirring from time to time.

Return the chicken to the pan and simmer for 5–6 minutes, or until the chicken is cooked through. Garnish with fresh coriander leaves, if you like.

Optional: Thai-style curries are typically quite runny. If you prefer a thicker sauce, stir in the optional cornflour slurry when the chicken is cooked and allow to bubble for 2 minutes, until the sauce has thickened.

QUICK COOK

VEGGIE

VEGAN

USE VEGGIE/
VEGAN 'BEEF'
STRIPS

**FREEZE
ME**

**DAIRY
FREE**

**GLUTEN
FREE**

USE GF SOY
SAUCE

BEEF, GINGER AND ORANGE STIR-FRY

🕐 **15 MINS**　　🍲 **10 MINS**　　✕ **SERVES 2**

PER SERVING:
266 KCAL /28G CARBS

low-calorie cooking spray
200g lean quick-cooking beef
　steak (we used rump), cut into
　strips
3 spring onions, trimmed and
　thinly sliced
1 red pepper, deseeded and
　thinly sliced
75g fine green beans, trimmed
2 garlic cloves, peeled and
　crushed
3cm (1¼in) piece of root ginger,
　peeled and grated
juice of 2 oranges
2 tbsp dark soy sauce
1 tbsp honey
1 tbsp rice vinegar
2 tsp cornflour
handful of fresh coriander,
　chopped

TO ACCOMPANY
50g nest of egg noodles per
　portion, cooked according to
　packet instructions (+ 171 kcal
　per serving)

When you're after a filling, flavoursome dinner in a flash, stir-fries never disappoint! To liven up the tender beef pieces and crunchy veggies in our dish, we've used freshly squeezed orange juice and kitchen cupboard staples to create an irresistibly zingy, takeaway-style sauce. It'll go from wok to plate in under 30 minutes, served over a bed of slurp-worthy noodles.

Weekly Indulgence

Place a wok or large frying pan over a high heat and spray with low-calorie cooking spray. When hot, tip in the beef strips and stir-fry for about 2 minutes, until browned and cooked to your liking. Remove from the pan and set aside.

Reduce the heat to medium and give the pan another spray of low-calorie cooking spray.

Reserve a sprinkling of sliced spring onion for garnishing and add the rest to the wok along with the peppers and green beans. Stir-fry for 5 minutes, then add the garlic and ginger and fry for a further minute. Add the orange juice, soy sauce, honey and rice vinegar.

Mix the cornflour with 1 tablespoon of cold water then quickly stir it into the pan when the sauce begins to bubble and keep stirring until it thickens.

Return the beef to the pan and stir in, along with the coriander (save some for garnish if you wish). Allow to heat through thoroughly.

Serve with noodles, garnished with the reserved spring onion and coriander.

TIP:

We enjoy our green beans with a bite to them. If you prefer a softer vegetable, allow the veggies to simmer in the sauce for a minute or two before thickening. Add a tablespoon or so of water, if the sauce reduces too much.

QUICK COOK

VEGGIE

USE VEGGIE
ITALIAN HARD
CHEESE

**FREEZE
ME**

**GLUTEN
FREE**

USE GF
SPAGHETTI

GARLIC, CHILLI AND PARSLEY SPAGHETTI

🕐 **10 MINS**   🍲 **10 MINS**   ✕ **SERVES 4**

PER SERVING:
332 KCAL /52G CARBS

300g dried spaghetti
low-calorie cooking spray
4 garlic cloves, peeled and finely
  chopped
1 small red chilli, deseeded and
  finely chopped
10g flat-leaf parsley, stalks
  removed and leaves chopped
60g Parmesan, finely grated
sea salt and freshly ground
  black pepper

Garlic lovers, this one's for you! With just a handful of budget-friendly ingredients and a spare 20 minutes, you can rustle up this punchy pasta dish. Beautifully simple, you'll be twisting up forkfuls of silky spaghetti in no time. It's medium-spicy from the chilli, although you can add more or less to suit your taste. Stir in some parsley for freshness and finish it off with a sprinkle of Parmesan.

Everyday Light

Put the spaghetti in a large saucepan of boiling water, then lower the heat and partially cover with a lid. Simmer for 10 minutes or until al dente. It will be ready when the spaghetti is tender when you bite a piece, but not too soft. Drain the spaghetti, saving 200ml of the pasta cooking water.

Return the spaghetti to the pan, putting the lid on to keep it warm. Set aside, off the heat.

Spray a large, deep, non-stick frying pan with low-calorie cooking spray and place over a low-medium heat. Add the garlic and chilli and cook gently for about 2 minutes or until the garlic is lightly golden. Take care not to overcook the garlic as it can burn easily.

Add the drained spaghetti to the frying pan with about 150ml of the reserved pasta cooking water and stir well to combine. The mixture should be glossy and moist. Add a little more of the cooking water if needed. Stir in the parsley and season with salt and pepper.

Remove from the heat and serve sprinkled with the grated Parmesan.

The dish will keep in the fridge for up to 1–2 days. To freeze, follow standard guidelines for defrosting and reheating.

TIP:
Try adding diced cooked bacon, ham or cooked chicken to this dish.

CARROT AND GINGER SOUP

🕐 **15 MINS**   🍲 **35 MINS**   ✕ **SERVES 4**

VEGGIE

VEGAN
USE VEGAN
STOCK CUBES

FREEZE
ME

BATCH
COOK

DAIRY
FREE

GLUTEN
FREE
USE GF STOCK
CUBES

PER SERVING:
122 KCAL /19G CARBS

low-calorie cooking spray
750g carrots, peeled and sliced
1 onion, peeled and roughly
    chopped
2 garlic cloves, peeled and
    crushed
5cm (2in) piece of root ginger,
    peeled and grated
1.2 litres vegetable stock
    (2 vegetable stock cubes
    dissolved in 1.2 litres boiling
    water)
grated zest of 1 orange
1 tbsp light soy sauce
small handful of fresh coriander
    leaves, chopped

TO ACCOMPANY (OPTIONAL)
60g wholemeal bread rolls
    (+ 146 kcal per roll)

Warming lunches don't come much lighter than this Carrot and Ginger Soup. Pairing fresh ginger with carrot brings a little bit of heat to cut through the natural sweetness of the vegetables. You'll love how easy this recipe is to batch cook, so you can freeze individual portions for a later date. At just 122 calories per serving, we'd recommend dishing it up with a crusty wholemeal roll to mop up every last drop.

Everyday Light

Spray a large saucepan with low-calorie cooking spray and place over a medium heat. Add the carrots and onion and cook for 5 minutes, until beginning to soften, then add the garlic and ginger and cook for another minute. Add the stock and orange zest, bring to the boil then turn down the heat and simmer for 30 minutes until the carrots are soft.

Add the soy sauce and coriander and blitz in a food processor or with a stick blender until smooth.

This soup is quite thick. If you prefer it thinner, add a little water until it is the consistency you prefer.

The soup will keep in the fridge for up to 3 days. To freeze, follow standard guidelines for defrosting and reheating.

VEGGIE

VEGAN
USE RAMEN NOODLES

FREEZE ME
BROTH ONLY

BATCH COOK

DAIRY FREE

GLUTEN FREE
USE GF NOODLES AND SOY SAUCE

PEANUT RAMEN

🕐 **10 MINS**　🍲 **10 MINS**　✕ **SERVES 2**

PER SERVING:
304 KCAL / 38G CARBS

low-calorie cooking spray
2 garlic cloves, peeled and crushed
1.5cm (¾in) piece of root ginger, peeled and finely grated
½ tbsp curry powder
250ml vegetable stock (1 vegetable stock cube dissolved in 250ml boiling water)
400ml coconut plant-based drink
1 lime, half juiced, the other half cut into wedges for garnish
2 tbsp light soy sauce
2 tbsp peanut butter powder, mixed to a paste with 2 tbsp water
1 pak choi, sliced
50g baby corn, cut into thirds
50g mangetout
125g long-stem broccoli
50g nest of dried egg noodles
handful of fresh coriander leaves, chopped
2 spring onions, thinly sliced
1 chilli, thinly sliced, to garnish (optional)

If satay chicken is your go-to takeaway order, our Peanut Ramen will be up your street. A super satisfying lunch or light dinner, this nutty broth is ready in just 20 minutes! Best described as a satay-noodle-style soup, you can bulk it out with fried tofu pieces or another nest of noodles if you're feeling extra hungry. At 304 calories per bowlful, there's room to make it your own with your favourite ramen toppings!

Everyday Light ———————————

Spray a wok or large saucepan with low-calorie cooking spray and place over a medium heat. Add the garlic and ginger and fry for 2 minutes, then add the curry powder and cook for a further minute. Add the stock, coconut drink, lime juice and soy sauce and whisk in the peanut paste. Bring to the boil then add the pak choi, baby corn, mangetout and broccoli. Cook for 5 minutes.

At this point the broth (minus the noodles) can be frozen. (Defrost overnight in the fridge, reheat in a microwave or in a saucepan on the hob until piping hot, and add cooked noodles just before serving.)

Meanwhile, cook the noodles in a separate pan of boiling water for 1 minute less than the packet instructions (this will usually be about 3 minutes). Drain.

Add the drained noodles to the peanut and vegetable broth and cook for another minute until the noodles are fully cooked.

Divide between bowls and top with the coriander, spring onions, sliced chilli (if using) and serve!

FREEZE ME

BATCH COOK

DAIRY FREE

USE DF CHEESE

GLUTEN FREE

USE GF SANDWICH THINS

PIZZA POCKETS

🕐 **15 MINS**   🍲 **10 MINS**   ✕ **SERVES 6**

PER SERVING:
167 KCAL /23G CARBS

3 tbsp tomato puree
½ tsp white granulated sweetener
½ tsp garlic granules
¾ tsp dried mixed herbs
6 sliced soft white or brown sandwich thins
½ pepper (any colour), deseeded and diced
20g sliced pepperoni, diced
20g reduced-fat mozzarella, grated
20g reduced-fat mature Cheddar, grated
1 medium egg, beaten

TO ACCOMPANY (OPTIONAL)
75g mixed salad (+ 15 kcal per serving)

A savoury bake you can get creative with, these Pizza Pockets really are what you make of them! We've used classic pepperoni pizza as the inspiration behind our filling, so there's nothing to stop you throwing your favourite pizzeria-inspired toppings into the mix (adjusting the calories accordingly). You don't want the tomato sauce or gloriously gooey mozzarella to escape, so be sure to tightly seal the edges of your sandwich-thin 'crust' before baking!

Everyday Light ───────────────

Preheat the oven to 200°C (fan 180°C/gas mark 6) and line a baking tray with non-stick baking paper.

In a small bowl, mix the tomato puree, sweetener, garlic granules and ½ teaspoon of the mixed herbs with 2 tablespoons of cold water until smooth.

Split the sandwich thins in half and lay out on a chopping board. Spread a little of the tomato sauce mixture onto the inside of both the top and bottom halves of each sandwich thin, leaving a 1cm (½in) border around the edges. Divide the peppers and pepperoni between the bottom sections of the sandwich thins. Sprinkle over the mozzarella and Cheddar.

Brush beaten egg around the edge and place one of the sandwich thin lids on top of the filling. Press the centre of the lid down gently with a flat hand, then press around the edges to seal. Use a fork to crimp the edges and seal well. Repeat until you've made all 6.

Place onto the lined baking tray and brush all over with the remaining egg. Sprinkle over the remaining mixed herbs and bake in the oven for 10 minutes or until golden brown.

Remove from the oven and place on a wire rack. You can serve these hot or cold, but we prefer them hot. Serve with a mixed salad or other accompaniment of your choice.

The pockets will keep in the fridge for 3 days. To freeze, follow standard guidelines for defrosting and reheat in the oven at 200°C (fan 180°C/gas mark 6) until piping hot throughout.

VEGGIE

USE VEGETARIAN
BACON AND
VEGETARIAN
ITALIAN HARD
CHEESE

**FREEZE
ME**

**BATCH
COOK**

**GLUTEN
FREE**

USE GF
BREADCRUMBS
AND STOCK
CUBE

CAULIFLOWER CHEESE WITH BACON

🕐 **10 MINS**　🍲 **15 MINS**　✕ **SERVES 4**

PER SERVING:
288 KCAL / 28G CARBS

SPECIAL EQUIPMENT
18 x 27cm (7 x 10½in)
ovenproof dish

600g cauliflower, trimmed and
　cut into medium-sized florets
low-calorie cooking spray
6 smoked bacon medallions, cut
　into 1–2cm (½–¾in) dice

FOR THE CHEESE SAUCE
250ml skimmed milk
250ml vegetable stock (1 low-
　salt vegetable stock cube
　dissolved in 250ml boiling
　water)
2 tbsp cornflour
½ tsp onion granules
½ tsp garlic granules
1 tsp Dijon mustard
150g reduced-fat spreadable
　cheese
15g Parmesan, finely grated
15g panko breadcrumbs
freshly ground black pepper

TO ACCOMPANY (OPTIONAL)
80g steamed green vegetables
　(+ 38 kcal per serving)

Imagine your favourite cheesy side dish, but better! With crispy bites of bacon and a crunchy, golden, breadcrumb topping, this is the ultimate cauliflower cheese recipe. Despite the indulgent-tasting cheese sauce, it's nice and low in calories, and it's ready to eat in just 25 minutes. Too good to only enjoy as a side dish, we love to plate up a serving of creamy cauli for dinner, with extra steamed vegetables on the side.

Everyday Light ──────────────────

Put the cauliflower florets in a large saucepan of boiling water and cover with a lid. Cook for 5–6 minutes, or until the cauliflower is tender, taking care not to overcook otherwise it will become mushy – insert a sharp knife into the thickest part of a cauliflower stalk to test if it is tender. Drain well and spread out evenly in the ovenproof dish.

Spray a small frying pan with low-calorie cooking spray and place over a medium heat. Add the diced bacon and cook for 4–5 minutes, or until crispy round the edges. Scatter the bacon over the cauliflower in the ovenproof dish.

Pour the milk and stock into a saucepan and heat until just boiling. Mix the cornflour with 2 tablespoons of cold water and stir until smooth. Stir the cornflour slurry into the hot liquid, stirring constantly with a wooden spoon or balloon whisk, and simmer for 3–4 minutes, or until thickened slightly.

Reduce the heat and stir in the onion and garlic granules, mustard, spreadable cheese and half the Parmesan, and season with black pepper. Pour the cheese sauce evenly over the cauliflower and bacon in the ovenproof dish. Top with the remaining Parmesan and the panko breadcrumbs and place under a preheated medium grill for about 5 minutes, or until golden brown and bubbling. Serve hot, alone, or with steamed vegetables or an accompaniment of your choice.

TIPS:

We found the bacon made this dish salty enough, so we only seasoned with black pepper.
Use a spreadable cheese with a strong Cheddar flavour.

PIZZA PORK

🕐 **10 MINS** 🍲 **15 MINS** ✕ **SERVES 4**

PER SERVING:
288 KCAL /4.6G CARBS

low-calorie cooking spray
4 pork steaks or chops, approx.
  110g each, all visible fat
  removed
½ medium red onion, peeled and
  finely chopped
½ red pepper, deseeded and
  finely chopped
2 tbsp ready-made green pesto
2 tbsp reduced-fat cream
  cheese
40g reduced-fat mature
  Cheddar, finely grated
½ tsp garlic granules
4 cherry tomatoes, quartered
sea salt and freshly ground
  black pepper

FOR THE TOP
20g reduced-fat mature
  Cheddar, finely grated
a few small fresh basil leaves, to
  garnish (optional)

TO ACCOMPANY (OPTIONAL)
80g steamed mixed vegetables
  (+ 38 kcal per serving)

Next time you're craving pizza, make this instead! We've turned humble pork steaks into a flavour-packed dinner with a bubbling, cheesy, pizza-inspired topping. From start to finish, these take just 25 minutes to make, so they're speedy enough to rustle up even on busy weeknights. Feel free to get creative with your toppings (adjusting the calories as necessary)! You can experiment with different vegetable combinations and we promise they'll be delicious every time.

Everyday Light ────────────────────

Preheat the grill to a high setting and spray a baking tray with low-calorie cooking spray.

Season the pork steaks with a little salt and pepper, place on the baking tray and pop under the grill, turning occasionally until cooked through. This will take about 8 minutes, but may take a little more or less depending on the thickness of your pork steaks.

While the pork is cooking, spray a small frying pan with low-calorie cooking spray and place over a medium heat. Add the onion and pepper and cook for 5–6 minutes until softened and beginning to turn golden.

Transfer the cooked onion and peppers to a mixing bowl. Add the pesto, cream cheese, Cheddar and garlic granules. Season well with salt and pepper, then stir until combined.

When the pork steaks are cooked, remove from under the grill and reduce the grill heat to medium. Spread the pesto mixture evenly over the pork steaks in a thick layer. Place the tomatoes on top and sprinkle with the extra Cheddar. Place back under the grill for 5 minutes until the topping is bubbling and golden.

Scatter a few basil leaves over the top (if using) and serve with an accompaniment of your choice.

TIP:
Try adding other vegetables of your choice, such as a few sliced mushrooms or spring onions.

TUNA MELT WRAP

🕐 **10 MINS**   🗑 **4 MINS**   ✕ **SERVES 4**

PER SERVING:
131 KCAL /12G CARBS

1 x 145g tin tuna in brine, drained well

¼ small red onion, peeled and finely diced

25g reduced-fat cream cheese

1 tsp lemon juice

small pinch of cayenne pepper (optional)

2 low-calorie soft tortilla wraps

20g reduced-fat Cheddar slice, cut in half

20g Gouda slice, cut in half

4 slices of tomato

low-calorie cooking spray

sea salt and freshly ground black pepper

TO ACCOMPANY

75g mixed salad (+ 15 kcal per serving)

This Tuna Melt Wrap is a lifesaver when you're after a quick, slimming-friendly lunch or snack! Our simple, tasty filling makes the most of readily available ingredients; we've taken it up a notch with reduced-fat cream cheese and a little cayenne pepper. You'll know your melt is ready to serve with a mixed salad when your tortilla is crispy with gooey, Gouda cheese in the middle.

Everyday Light

Place the tuna chunks in a small mixing bowl and stir to break it up. Stir in the onion, cream cheese, lemon juice and cayenne pepper (if using), until well combined. Season well with salt and pepper.

Place the soft tortilla wraps on a chopping board. Divide the tuna mixture in half and spread over one half of each wrap. Place half a slice of Cheddar and half a slice of Gouda cheese, in a single layer, on top of the tuna mixture on each wrap. Place two slices of tomato on top of each layer of cheese. Fold the wrap over the filling on each, to make two semi-circular Tuna Melt Wraps.

Spray a large frying pan with low-calorie cooking spray and place over a medium heat. When the pan is hot, lift the Tuna Melts into the frying pan using a fish slice. Press down slightly with the fish slice and cook for about 2 minutes on each side, until lightly browned and the cheese is melting inside.

Cut each Tuna Melt Wrap in half. Serve at once with a crisp mixed salad.

TIPS:

We use a mixture of Cheddar and Gouda to help give a bit of a cheesy 'pull', but just use Cheddar if you prefer. Or experiment with other cheeses such as mozzarella. We use ready-sliced cheese that comes in packs and is available in most supermarkets.
We added a small pinch of cayenne pepper to our mixture for a hint of spice, but you can leave this out if you prefer.

VEGGIE

USE VEGGIE
ITALIAN HARD
CHEESE

VEGAN

USE VEGAN
ITALIAN HARD
CHEESE

DAIRY
FREE

USE DF ITALIAN
HARD CHEESE

LOW
CARB

GLUTEN
FREE

USE GF STOCK
CUBES

ROASTED LEMON AND PARMESAN BROCCOLI

🕐 **5 MINS**   🍲 **12–18 MINS**   ✕ **SERVES 4**

PER SERVING:
57 KCAL /3G CARBS

low-calorie cooking spray
juice of ½ lemon
1 garlic clove, peeled and
   crushed
350g head of broccoli
20g Parmesan, finely grated
sea salt and freshly ground
   black pepper

If you always boil or steam your broccoli, it's time to try roasting it! Baked in the oven, the florets turn crisp and golden on the outside, and tender in the middle, with a nice charred flavour that's hard to beat. Tossed in lemon juice and finished with salty Parmesan cheese, these gorgeous greens go especially well with Italian-inspired main courses. Why not serve this recipe as a side dish to the Garlic, Chilli and Parsley Spaghetti that you'll find on page 58?

Everyday Light

Preheat the oven to 220°C (fan 200°C/gas mark 7) and spray a baking tray with low-calorie cooking spray.

Mix the lemon juice and garlic together in a large mixing bowl.

Trim the woody stem off the broccoli, cut the head into bite-sized florets and place in the bowl with the lemon juice and garlic. Season with a little salt (not too much as the Parmesan is salty) and some black pepper. Toss to coat the florets.

Scatter the florets evenly over the sprayed baking tray, making sure you don't overcrowd the tray. This will ensure even cooking. Spray with more low-calorie cooking spray, place in the oven and roast for 12–18 minutes. Check regularly, as the broccoli can catch and burn and become bitter. When cooked, the broccoli should be brown and crispy around the edges and tender in the middle.

Sprinkle over the Parmesan and serve!

VEGGIE

VEGAN

DAIRY FREE

GLUTEN FREE

USE GF SOY SAUCE

STICKY PINEAPPLE FRIED RICE

🕐 **10 MINS** 🍲 **15 MINS** ✕ **SERVES 2**

PER SERVING:
358 KCAL /66G CARBS

1 tsp sesame seeds
low-calorie cooking spray
1 red pepper, deseeded and diced
4 spring onions, trimmed, thinly sliced and separated into white and green slices
150g fresh pineapple, peeled, cored and cut into 1cm (½in) dice
1 red chilli, deseeded and finely chopped (leave seeds in if you would like it hotter)
2 garlic cloves, peeled and crushed
250g pouch of cooked jasmine rice
75g frozen peas, cooked according to packet instructions
2 tbsp light soy sauce
1 lime, half juiced, the other half cut into wedges for garnish
2 tsp vegetarian fish sauce
1 tsp white granulated sweetener or sugar
sea salt and freshly ground black pepper
lime wedges, to serve (optional)

When you need a speedy side dish, this sticky, sweet and savoury fried rice is hard to beat. On the table in 25 minutes, it's so easy to turn a simple pouch of cooked jasmine rice into this Thai-inspired dish. You can cook your own jasmine rice if you prefer, but it can be tricky to get that fluffy yet sticky texture just right. Our stress-free recipe is finished with a sprinkle of toasted sesame seeds and sliced spring onions to add fresh, tangy flavours to your fakeaway night.

Special Occasion

Place a dry large frying pan or wok over a medium heat. When hot, add the sesame seeds and toast for 3–4 minutes, stirring until they turn golden brown. Keep a close eye on them so they don't burn, remove from the pan and set aside.

Spray the pan with low-calorie cooking spray, add the red pepper and white spring onion slices (reserve the green slices for later) and cook for 2–3 minutes. Add the pineapple, chilli and garlic and continue to cook for a further 5 minutes. Add the cooked jasmine rice and cooked peas, then cook for 2–3 minutes.

In a small bowl, mix the soy sauce, lime juice, vegetarian fish sauce and sweetener, until the sweetener has dissolved, then add to the pan. Stir through and continue to cook until the liquid has evaporated or has been absorbed and the rice is piping hot. Taste and season with a little salt and pepper if needed.

Divide between two plates, sprinkle over the green spring onion slices and toasted sesame seeds and serve with lime wedges, if you like!

TIP:
To turn this into a more substantial meal, fry some diced chicken breast along with the onions, and scramble in an egg at the end of step 4.

TUNA BEAN SALAD

🕐 **5 MINS**   🍲 **NO COOK**   ✕ **SERVES 4**

PER SERVING:
96 KCAL /10G CARBS

1 x 400g tin cannellini beans in
water, rinsed and drained
1 x 145g tin tuna in water,
drained
¼ small red onion, peeled and
thinly sliced
100g cherry tomatoes,
quartered
1 small garlic clove, peeled and
crushed
8g flat-leaf parsley, stalks
removed and leaves roughly
chopped
1 tbsp lemon juice
2 squirts light olive oil spray
sea salt and freshly ground
black pepper

A vibrant, colourful lunch or summery side dish, this Tuna
Bean Salad is a real mood-booster! With a handful of fresh
ingredients including cannellini beans and tuna, there's
no shortage of protein to leave you feeling full long after
your final forkful. We've livened up the flavours with garlic
and parsley, and tossed everything together with a tangy
drizzle of lemon juice and olive oil.

Everyday Light _____

Place the cannellini beans, tuna, red onion, tomatoes, garlic
and parsley in a medium bowl and stir to combine. Add the
lemon juice, a couple of squirts of light olive oil and season
to taste with salt and pepper.

Toss the salad a little to mix, then serve as a side salad.

TIPS:

We've used a light olive
oil spray in this salad. It
has more calories, but
don't be tempted to use
low-calorie cooking spray;
it just won't be the same
in a salad!
You can try adding other
proteins to this salad
instead of tuna, if you
prefer. Cooked chicken,
cooked ham or cheese
such as feta would work
well – adjust the calories
accordingly.

QUICK COOK

FREEZE ME

DAIRY FREE
USE DF CHEESE AND MILK

GLUTEN FREE
USE GF PASTRY

BACON, CHEESE AND TOMATO SLICES

🕐 **15 MINS**　🍲 **15 MINS**　✕ **MAKES 16**

PER SERVING:
145 KCAL / 12G CARBS

low-calorie cooking spray
4 smoked bacon medallions, cut into 1cm (½in) dice
160g reduced-fat mature Cheddar, finely grated
½ tsp dried mixed herbs
1 tsp garlic granules
1 medium egg, beaten
375g ready-rolled light puff pastry sheet, about 40 x 26cm (16 x 10in)
12 cherry tomatoes, quartered
1 tsp skimmed milk, for glazing
sea salt and freshly ground black pepper

TO ACCOMPANY
75g crisp mixed salad
(+ 15 kcal per serving)

TIPS:

We find it's best to use the pastry straight from the fridge, depending on the brand you use. Some brands can be stickier than others and may become difficult to work with if they become warm, so we recommend using it chilled.
Make sure to grate the cheese finely as this helps it to go a long way.
You could substitute the bacon with cooked ham, if you prefer, adjusting the calories accordingly.

If you're flicking through on the hunt for savoury snacks, stop now! By using lean bacon, reduced-fat Cheddar and light puff pastry, we've cut the calories without compromising on the bakery-inspired flavours you know and love. Enjoy them as a snack, or pair them with a crisp, mixed salad for an easy, fun lunch.

Everyday Light ───────────────

Preheat the oven to 200°C (fan 180°C/gas mark 6) and line two large baking trays with non-stick baking paper.

Spray a small frying pan with low-calorie cooking spray and place over a medium heat. Add the bacon and fry for 3–4 minutes, until cooked. Drain on kitchen towel.

Place the cooked bacon in a medium bowl with the cheese, mixed herbs, garlic granules, beaten egg and season with salt and pepper, if needed. Taste before adding salt as you may find the bacon makes the mixture salty enough. Mix with a fork to form a stiff paste and set aside.

Unroll the pastry sheet, leaving it on the greaseproof paper packing, and place it on a work surface. Cut into 16 rectangles, each 6.5 x 10cm (2½ x 4in) in size. Place 8 pastry rectangles on each lined baking tray, leaving space between. Use a sharp knife to score a border around each rectangle, 1cm (½in) in from the edge, taking care not to cut right through. Prick the middle part of each rectangle with a fork.

Divide the cheese and bacon mixture between the pastry rectangles, leaving the border around the edges. Push down a little and spread out with a fork to cover the middle section. Place three tomato pieces on top of each. Brush the edges with a little milk and bake in the oven for 10–12 minutes, until golden and slightly puffy. Serve hot or cold with a crisp mixed salad or other accompaniment of choice.

The slices will keep in the fridge for 1–2 days. To freeze, place in a freezerproof container interleaved with sheets of non-stick baking paper to prevent the slices sticking together. Follow standard guidelines for defrosting and reheat in the oven at 200°C (fan 180°C/gas mark 6) until piping hot throughout.

QUICK COOK

78

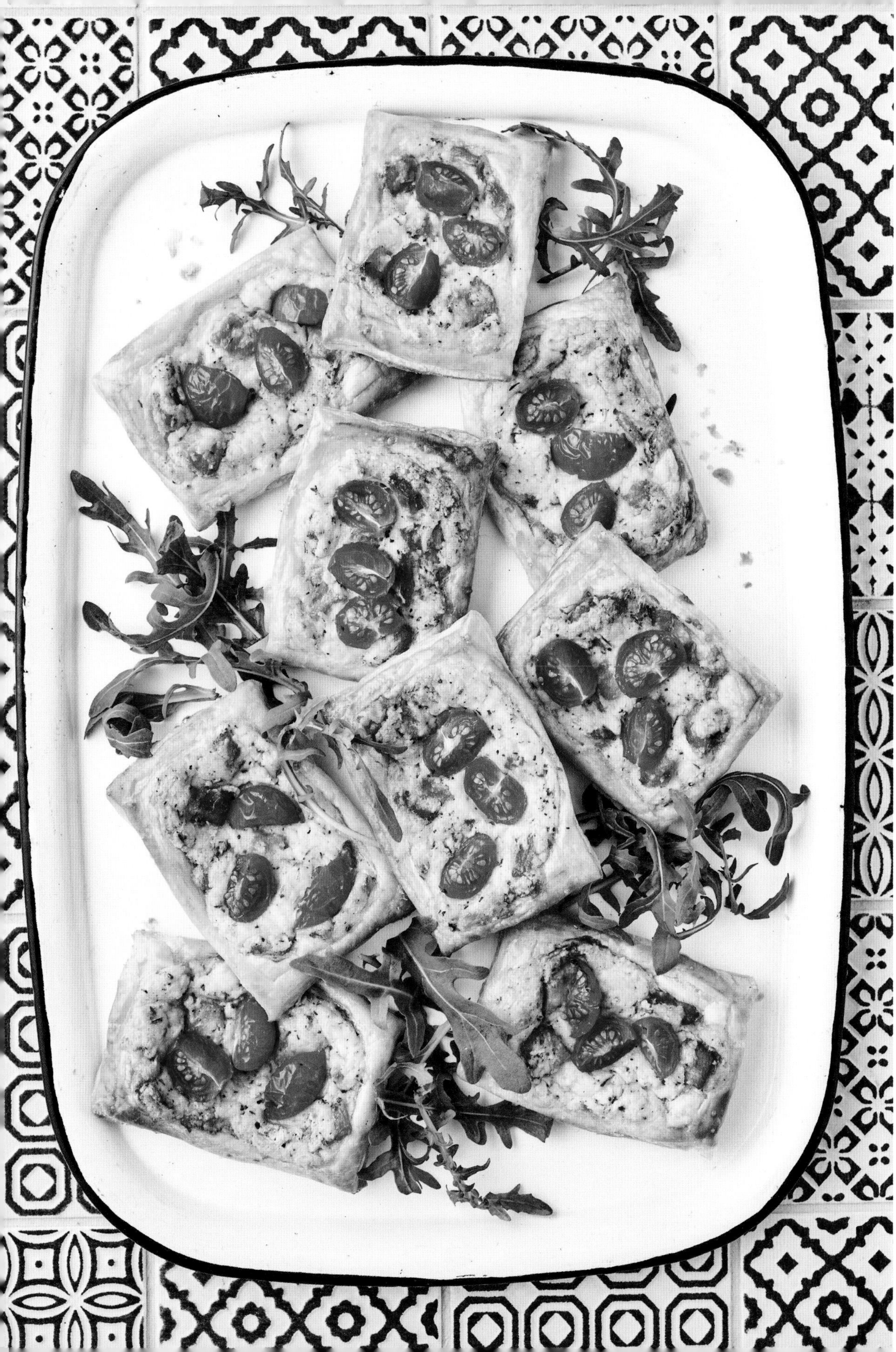

BLACK FOREST BAKEWELLS

⏱ **20 MINS**　🍲 **15 MINS**　✕ **MAKES 10**

VEGGIE

DAIRY FREE
USE DF SPREAD

LOW CARB

PER BAKEWELL:
80 KCAL /12G CARBS

SPECIAL EQUIPMENT
12-hole bun tin, 10cm (4in) plain round pastry cutter

low-calorie cooking spray
2 sheets (about 90g) of filo pastry
1 tbsp skimmed milk, for brushing
1 tbsp reduced-sugar cherry jam
10 fresh black cherries, stoned and halved
25g self-raising flour
25g reduced-fat spread
1 medium egg
2 tbsp white granulated sweetener
1 tsp cocoa powder
a few drops of almond extract
½ tsp icing sugar, for dusting

One bite of these Black Forest Bakewells and you'll be wondering where they've been all your life. This dreamy two-in-one recipe combines the rich, chocolatey sponge of a Black Forest gateau with the crisp pastry of a Bakewell tart. It's the ultimate combination of chocolate and cherries, with a hint of almond added in for good measure. You'd never know they're so low in calories!

Everyday Light

Preheat the oven to 200°C (fan 180°C/gas mark 6) and lightly grease ten holes of the 12-hole bun tin with a little low-calorie cooking spray.

Use the pastry cutter to cut out 20 circles from the filo pastry sheets. Brush the first circle with a little milk and press into the first hole in the bun tin, dry side down. Place a second circle of pastry on top and press into the hole to form a tart case. Repeat with the other nine holes of the bun tin until you've made ten tart cases.

Place in the oven and bake blind for about 5 minutes or until lightly golden, to ensure the bottom of the tart cases will be crisp.

Remove from the oven and allow them to cool slightly for a few minutes, then brush inside the bases with the jam. Place a cherry half in each tart case.

Put the flour, reduced-fat spread, egg, sweetener, cocoa powder and almond extract into a mixing bowl and mix for a minute or two using an electric hand mixer or wooden spoon.

Divide the mixture evenly between the ten tart cases and place another cherry half on top of each, cut side down. Bake in the oven for about 10 minutes, or until the sponge has risen and is firm and springy to the touch.

Remove the tarts from the bun tin and place on a wire rack to cool, then dust with a little icing sugar and serve.

SWEET TREATS

VEGGIE

VEGAN

FREEZE
ME

BATCH
COOK

DAIRY
FREE

GLUTEN
FREE

**USE GF PUFF
PASTRY**

APRICOT DANISH-STYLE PASTRIES

🕐 **10 MINS**   🍲 **15 MINS**   ✕ **MAKES 8**

PER SERVING:
118 KCAL /15G CARBS

200g ready-rolled light puff
pastry sheet, cut into eight
8cm (3¼in) squares
2 tinned apricot halves in fruit
juice, well-drained and cut into
quarters
1 tbsp flaked almonds, roughly
chopped
2 tbsp reduced-sugar apricot
jam

Who says pastry has to be off the slimming menu? We've
taken inspiration from Danish high-street bakeries to put
together these impressive little apricot treats. To keep the
calories down, we've paired crispy, light puff pastry with a
sweet centre of apricot and reduced-sugar jam. Quick and
simple to make and even easier to store, keep them in the
fridge or freezer ready to level-up your morning brew!

Everyday Light ————————————————

Preheat the oven to 220°C (fan 200°C/gas mark 7) and line
a large baking tray with a sheet of non-stick baking paper.

Place the pastry squares on the lined baking tray, leaving
space between each. Use a sharp knife to make four
diagonal cuts on each square, starting from the four corners,
towards the centre. Stop cutting about 1cm (½in) from the
centre. Each pastry square should now look like a square
containing four 'triangular' sections joined in the middle.

Take a corner of one of the 'triangular' sections and fold
into the centre. Press down. Repeat with the three remaining
'triangular' sections and press down firmly in the centre to
form a windmill or pinwheel shape. Repeat until you have
made 8 pastries.

Place an apricot piece in the centre of each pastry and
press down lightly. Bake for 10–12 minutes, until slightly risen,
crisp and golden brown. Remove from the oven and transfer
to a cooling rack.

Place the almonds on the baking tray and bake in the oven
for 2–3 minutes, until lightly golden. Watch carefully as the
almonds can burn easily. Remove from the oven and set aside.

Place the jam in a small microwave-safe bowl and
microwave for 15–20 seconds, until melted. Sieve the jam to
remove any bits. Brush the warm jam over the pastries to
glaze, and sprinkle with the toasted flaked almonds.

They will keep in the fridge for up to 3 days. If freezing,
defrost in the fridge and serve cold or reheat in a warm
oven for 4–5 minutes for a freshly baked taste. They aren't
suitable for reheating in the microwave.

TIPS:

You don't have to sprinkle
almonds on the tops
of the pastries if you'd
prefer not to. Without the
almonds, each pastry will
contain 110 kcal and 15g
of carbohydrates.
Make sure to assemble
the pastries once the
pastry pinwheels are on
the baking tray! It's more
difficult to lift them onto
the tray once made.

VEGGIE

VEGAN

USE VEGAN PROSECCO

DAIRY FREE

GLUTEN FREE

PEACH BELLINI JELLIES

🕐 **10 MINS**   🍲 **5 MINS**   ✕ **SERVES 6**

* PLUS 1–2 HOURS CHILLING

PER SERVING:
150 KCAL /20G CARBS

SPECIAL EQUIPMENT
6 x wine or dessert glasses

1 x 410g tin peaches in juice
550ml prosecco, at room temperature
2 tbsp white granulated sweetener
2 x 6.5g sachets vegetarian powdered gelatine
50ml peach schnapps (optional)
1 fresh peach, stoned and sliced, to decorate

TO ACCOMPANY (OPTIONAL)
swirl (12.5g) of low-fat aerosol cream (+ 24 kcal per serving)

Inspired by sunny Italian holidays, our Peach Bellini Jellies are a gorgeous grown-up treat. Combining jelly with juicy, sweet peaches, bubbly Prosecco and schnapps, each glass contains the easiest trip to the beach you'll ever take, for only 150 calories per serving! A dessert you can raise a toast with, they're the perfect way to round off an extra-special dinner.

Everyday Light —————————————————

Place the tinned peaches and their juice into a blender and blitz until they form a smooth puree.

Transfer into a saucepan. Whisk in 200ml of the prosecco, along with the granulated sweetener and the gelatine. Place over a medium heat and continue whisking until the sweetener and gelatine have dissolved. Keep whisking until the peach puree comes to the boil, then remove from the heat and quickly whisk in the remaining prosecco and peach schnapps (if using).

Pour into 6 individual glasses, cover and refrigerate for 1–2 hours until set.

Decorate with fresh peach slices and serve.

BANANA PANCAKE TRAYBAKE

🕐 **10 MINS**   🍲 **20 MINS**   ✕ **SERVES 8**

PER SERVING:
139 KCAL /26G CARBS

SPECIAL EQUIPMENT
24 x 24cm (9½ x 9½in) square baking tin

low-calorie cooking spray
200g self-raising flour
1 tsp baking powder
1 tbsp white granulated
    sweetener
200ml skimmed milk
1 medium egg
¼ tsp vanilla extract
1 medium banana, peeled and
    sliced
20g milk chocolate chips
¼ tsp icing sugar, for dusting

TO ACCOMPANY (OPTIONAL)
ready-made toffee-flavour
    dessert sauce (+ 17 kcal per tsp)

This Banana Pancake Traybake is so flipping good. From oven to plate in 20 minutes, you'd never be able to tell that these delightful squares are slimming friendly. They're made with a dreamy combo of sliced bananas and chocolate chips, but you can get creative and try different flavours each time. Enjoy as a snack, save for dessert and add a little dessert sauce or tuck into them at breakfast!

Everyday Light ─────────────────────

Preheat the oven to 180°C (fan 160°C/gas mark 4). Spray the baking tin with low-calorie cooking spray, grease thoroughly and then line the base and sides with non-stick baking paper.

Sift the flour and baking powder into a medium mixing bowl and stir in the sweetener.

In a measuring jug, mix together the milk, egg and vanilla extract and stir this wet mixture into the flour a little at a time until smooth. Beat together with a balloon whisk for 1–2 minutes.

Pour the mixture into the prepared tin, scatter over the banana slices and chocolate chips, and bake in the oven for 15–20 minutes, until the top is lightly golden brown.

Remove from the tin, remove the non-stick baking paper and cut into 8 squares. Dust with icing sugar and serve alone or drizzled with a little toffee-flavour dessert sauce.

RASPBERRY FILO TART

🕐 **15 MINS**   🍲 **10 MINS**   ✕ **SERVES 8**

PER SERVING:
168 KCAL /26G CARBS

SPECIAL EQUIPMENT
18cm (7in) round, loose-bottomed fluted metal flan tin

a little reduced-fat spread, for
  greasing
6 sheets of filo pastry
  (24cm/9½in squares)
1 medium egg, beaten
2 tbsp reduced-sugar seedless
  raspberry jam
50g reduced-fat cream cheese
25g chocolate nut spread
100g raspberries
¼ tsp icing sugar, for dusting

TO ACCOMPANY (OPTIONAL)
swirl (12.5g) of low-fat aerosol
  cream (+ 24 kcal per serving)

> **TIPS:**
> You could replace the
> raspberries with other soft
> fruit such as strawberries,
> blueberries, loganberries
> or blackberries if wished.
> Make sure to pat the
> fruit dry thoroughly with
> kitchen towel before
> placing in the pastry case
> otherwise they may make
> the pastry soggy.

Crunchy pastry, creamy chocolate and sweet raspberries – this easy dessert really has it all! Next time you fancy picking up a bakery treat, grab a pack of filo pastry instead and try this tart. Once you've baked the pastry into a crispy, golden case, you load it up with a mixture of smooth cream cheese and nutty chocolate spread, topped off with fresh raspberries to cut through the sweetness. Perfection!

Everyday Light ———————————————

Preheat the oven to 180° (fan 160°/gas mark 4) and thoroughly grease the flan tin with reduced-fat spread.

Evenly brush one side of the first sheet of filo pastry with beaten egg. Carefully lift and place the sheet, brushed-side up, in the base and up the sides of the flan tin, to form a crumpled-looking edge. Don't worry if the pastry tears, as you are aiming for a rustic-looking pastry case.

Repeat this process with the remaining 5 sheets of pastry, to line the flan tin and form the base and sides of the pastry case, finishing with the last sheet brushed-side up. Bake in the oven for about 10 minutes, or until crisp and golden.

Remove the pastry case from the oven, carefully remove it from the flan tin and leave to cool completely on a wire rack.

Place the jam in a small cup and stir until smooth and slackened a little. Use the back of a teaspoon to spread the jam evenly over the inside base of the cooled pastry case.

Place the cream cheese and chocolate nut spread in a small bowl and mix until smooth and completely blended. Spread the chocolate filling evenly over the jam layer using the back of a teaspoon. Place the raspberries in an even layer over the chocolate filling and dust with icing sugar.

Serve alone, with a swirl of aerosol cream or other accompaniment of your choice.

Quick COOK
↓
AIR FRYER *and* MULTI METHOD

VEGGIE

BATCH COOK

GLUTEN FREE

USE GF TORTILLA CHIPS

ZINGER HALLOUMI FRIES WITH GARLIC AND ONION DIP

🕐 **15 MINS**   🍲 **15 MINS**   ✕ **SERVES 4**

PER SERVING:
308 KCAL /25G CARBS

FOR THE FRIES
60g Doritos Chilli Heatwave
   flavour tortilla chips
2 tsp mild chilli powder
2 tsp garlic granules
2 tsp paprika
2 tsp onion granules
2 ½ tbsp cornflour
1 medium egg, beaten
200g reduced-fat halloumi,
   drained and cut into 1cm (½in)-
   wide fries
low-calorie cooking spray

FOR THE GARLIC AND ONION DIP
150g fat-free Greek-style
   yoghurt
½ tsp garlic granules
2 tsp lemon juice
1 spring onion, trimmed,
   green and white parts finely
   chopped
sea salt and freshly ground
   black pepper

TO ACCOMPANY
75g mixed salad
   (+ 15 kcal per serving)

These are halloumi fries but not as you know them! We've changed things up by giving them a crispy spiced coating and then oven-baked or air-fried them to keep the calories down. If you enjoy our Zinger Tuna Fishcakes, you'll love these as we've used the same crispy coating with a surprising ingredient – Chilli Heatwave Doritos. Serve with our Garlic and Onion Dip for perfect party nibbles!

Special Occasion ————————————————

OVEN METHOD

Preheat the oven to 220°C (fan 200°C/gas mark 7) and line a baking tray with a sheet of non-stick baking paper.

Put the Doritos, chilli powder, garlic granules, paprika and onion granules in a strong food bag. Squeeze out the air and seal the bag, then bash with a rolling pin or similar heavy object until the mixture resembles fine breadcrumbs. Tip the finely crushed mixture onto a plate and set aside.

Put the cornflour on a plate and the beaten egg on another plate. Dip the halloumi pieces in the cornflour, turning to lightly coat all over, then dip the floured halloumi pieces in the beaten egg, turning to thoroughly coat (handle the halloumi carefully when coating as it can be fragile once cut into fries). Finally, dip the halloumi pieces in the crispy coating mixture, turning to coat them completely.

Place the coated fries on the lined baking tray and spray with low-calorie cooking spray. Place in the preheated oven and bake for 10–15 minutes until crisp and golden.

While the fries are cooking, make the Garlic and Onion Dip. Place all the ingredients for the dip in a small bowl and mix well. Season to taste with salt and pepper.

Serve the fries hot with the dip and a crisp mixed salad.

Continued...

TIP:
You can add a little more chilli powder to make these spicier if you like.

AIR-FRYER METHOD
🍚 8 MINS

Preheat the air fryer for a few minutes at 190°C.

Put the Doritos, chilli powder, garlic granules, paprika and onion granules in a strong food bag. Squeeze out the air and seal the bag, then bash with a rolling pin or similar heavy object until the mixture resembles fine breadcrumbs. Tip the finely crushed mixture onto a plate and set aside.

Put the cornflour on a plate and the beaten egg on another plate. Dip the halloumi pieces in the cornflour, turning to lightly coat all over, then dip the floured halloumi pieces in the beaten egg, turning to thoroughly coat (handle the halloumi carefully when coating as it can be fragile once cut into fries). Finally, dip the halloumi pieces in the crispy coating mixture, turning to coat them completely.

Place the coated fries in the preheated air-fryer basket, leaving space between each, and spray with low-calorie cooking spray. You will probably need to cook the fries in two batches, depending on the size of your air fryer. Cook for about 8 minutes until crisp and golden.

While the fries are cooking, make the Garlic and Onion Dip. Place all the ingredients for the dip in a small bowl and mix well. Season to taste with salt and pepper.

Serve the fries hot with the dip, some crisp mixed salad.

TIP:
Why not try making these with different flavoured tortilla chips?

SWEET CHILLI CHICKEN NUGGETS

🕐 **10 MINS**   📦 **VARIABLE** (SEE BELOW)   ✕ **SERVES 4**

PER SERVING:
208 KCAL / 14G CARBS

2 medium slices of wholemeal bread (about 37g each)
1 tsp garlic granules
2 tsp mild chilli powder
1 medium egg, beaten
420g chicken breast (visible fat removed), cut into 3cm (1¼in) chunks
low-calorie cooking spray
3 tbsp ready-made reduced-sugar Thai sweet chilli sauce
2 spring onions, trimmed and finely chopped
sea salt and freshly ground black pepper

TO ACCOMPANY
75g mixed salad
(+ 15 kcal per serving)

We've given humble chicken nuggets a makeover with a sweet and spicy Thai-inspired twist! These mildly spiced, crisp golden nuggets are tossed in a little sweet chilli sauce and chopped spring onion to make a simple and tasty change! If you like things spicier, add more chilli powder to suit your own taste.

Everyday Light ────────────────

OVEN METHOD
📦 **30 MINUTES**

Preheat the oven to 200°C (fan 180°C/gas mark 6) and line a large baking tray with a sheet of non-stick baking paper.

Place the bread in a food processor and blitz to make fine breadcrumbs. You could also use a coarse grater to do this.

Place the breadcrumbs on a plate, add the garlic granules and chilli powder, and season well with salt and pepper. Mix with clean fingers until completely combined. Place the beaten egg on another plate. Dip the chicken pieces in the egg to coat all over, then into the breadcrumbs until completely coated. Place the coated chicken pieces in a single layer on the lined baking tray, leaving space between each one. Spray the tops with low-calorie cooking spray and bake in the oven for 15 minutes.

Turn the nuggets over and spray again, then return to the oven for a further 15 minutes until crisp and golden, making sure there are no signs of pinkness and the juices run clear.

Put the nuggets in a medium bowl and pour over the sweet chilli sauce. Toss to coat thoroughly in the sauce, then add the chopped spring onion and toss again until well combined. Serve at once with a mixed salad.

If freezing nuggets raw, freeze on a tray, then layer between sheets of non-stick baking paper in a suitable container. If freezing nuggets after cooking, layer between sheets of non-stick baking paper in a suitable container. Defrost in fridge before cooking or reheating. Then add sweet chilli sauce and spring onion.

Continued...

TIP:
Make sure to use fine garlic granules so they will stick to the chicken nuggets well.

AIR-FRYER METHOD
🍲 15 MINUTES

SPECIAL EQUIPMENT
Air fryer

Preheat the air fryer to 170°C.

Place the bread in a food processor and blitz to make fine breadcrumbs. You could also use a coarse grater to do this.

Place the breadcrumbs on a plate, add the garlic granules and chilli powder, and season well with salt and pepper. Mix with clean fingers until completely combined. Place the beaten egg on another plate. Dip the chicken pieces in the egg to coat all over, then into the breadcrumbs until completely coated. Place the coated chicken pieces in a single layer in the preheated air-fryer basket, leaving space between each one. (You may need to cook the nuggets in batches depending on the capacity of your air fryer.) Spray the tops with low-calorie cooking spray and cook for 15 minutes until crisp and golden, turning the nuggets over halfway through and spraying again. Make sure there are no signs of pinkness and the juices run clear.

Put the nuggets into a medium bowl and pour over the sweet chilli sauce. Toss to coat thoroughly in the sauce, then add the chopped spring onion and toss again until well combined. Serve at once with a mixed salad.

If freezing nuggets raw, freeze on a tray, then layer between sheets of non-stick baking paper in a suitable container. If freezing nuggets after cooking, layer between sheets of non-stick baking paper in a suitable container. Defrost in fridge before cooking or reheating. Then add sweet chilli sauce and spring onion.

PESTO CHICKEN ESCALOPE

 5 MINS   **VARIABLE** (SEE BELOW)   ✕ **SERVES 2**

PER SERVING:
277 KCAL /17G CARBS

2 medium skinless chicken
  breasts (visible fat removed),
  about 260g in total
3 tbsp reduced-fat green
  pesto sauce
1 tsp garlic granules
2 tsp lemon juice
40g panko breadcrumbs
low-calorie cooking spray
sea salt and freshly ground
  black pepper

TO ACCOMPANY
75g mixed salad
  (+ 15 kcal per serving)
(OPTIONAL)
120g boiled new potatoes
  (+ 90 kcal per serving)

A midweek dinner hero, these Pesto Chicken Escalopes are exactly what you want when you don't know what you fancy! Ready in 35 minutes (and only 25 minutes if you use your air fryer), they're really versatile and so tasty. Using shop-bought pesto cuts down on prep time and effortlessly ramps up the flavours. Crunchy on the outside and juicy in the middle, they're a crowd-pleaser every time.

Everyday Light ─────────────────────

OVEN METHOD
🍲 **30 MINS**

Preheat the oven to 220°C (fan 200°C/gas mark 7) and line a baking tray with non-stick baking parchment.

Place the two chicken breasts on a sheet of non-stick baking parchment on a chopping board and cover with a second sheet. Using a rolling pin or heavy pan, bash the chicken breasts until flat and about 2cm (¾in) thick.

In a small bowl, combine the pesto, garlic granules, lemon juice and a little salt and pepper and mix until smooth. Coat the two bashed chicken breasts on both sides with the pesto mixture.

Tip the panko breadcrumbs onto a plate and dip each chicken breast in the breadcrumbs, until coated on all sides.

Place onto the lined baking tray and spray the top of each chicken breast with low-calorie cooking spray. Bake in the oven for 30 minutes, turning the chicken breasts over halfway through. The chicken is cooked through when the juices run clear and there are no signs of pinkness.

Serve with a mixed salad, and some new potatoes if you like.

If freezing, cool as quickly as possible, then layer between sheets of non-stick baking paper before freezing in a container. Reheat in the oven at 220°C (fan 200°C/gas mark 7) until crisp and piping hot throughout.

Continued...

AIR FRYER METHOD
🍲 20 MINS

SPECIAL EQUIPMENT
Air fryer

Preheat the air fryer to 180°C.

Place the two chicken breasts on a sheet of non-stick baking parchment on a chopping board and cover with a second sheet. Using a rolling pin or heavy pan, bash the chicken breasts until flat and about 2cm (¾in) thick.

In a small bowl, combine the pesto, garlic granules, lemon juice and a little salt and pepper and mix until smooth. Coat the two bashed chicken breasts on both sides with the pesto mixture.

Tip the panko breadcrumbs onto a plate and dip each chicken breast in the breadcrumbs, until coated on all sides.

Place into the air-fryer basket and spray the top of each chicken breast with low-calorie cooking spray. Cook for 20 minutes, turning the chicken breasts over halfway through. The chicken is cooked through when the juices run clear and there are no signs of pinkness.

Serve with a mixed salad, and some new potatoes if you like.

FIERY CHILLI CHICKEN KEBABS

⏱ **5 MINS**　📷 **VARIABLE** (SEE BELOW)　✕ **SERVES 4**

PER SERVING:
193 KCAL /12G CARBS

SPECIAL EQUIPMENT
4 x wooden or metal skewers

2 tbsp soy sauce
2 tbsp honey
4 tsp sriracha sauce
2 tsp chilli powder
2 tsp reduced-sugar ketchup
½ tsp garlic granules
½ tsp dried chilli flakes
500g skinless, boneless chicken
　thigh fillets, all visible fat
　removed, cut into chunks

TO SERVE
1 spring onion, trimmed and
　thinly sliced
½ tsp dried chilli flakes
lime slices (optional)

TO ACCOMPANY
75g mixed salad (+ 15 kcal per
　serving)

With sriracha, chilli powder and chilli flakes in the marinade, we've made sure these juicy chicken kebabs live up to their fiery name. They don't take long to cook, but it's well worth preparing them in advance, so you can give them plenty of time to marinate. Big flavour for hardly any effort, you can cook these in the oven or pop them in the air fryer if you want to save even more time.

Everyday Light ──────────────

OVEN METHOD

In a bowl, combine the soy sauce, honey, sriracha sauce, chilli powder, tomato ketchup, garlic granules and chilli flakes. Add the chicken and stir to coat. Cover and pop into the fridge for an hour to marinate.

Preheat the oven to 200°C (fan 180°C/gas mark 6).

Once the chicken has marinated, thread the meat evenly onto 4 skewers. Place the kebabs on a baking tray and cook in the oven for 30–35 minutes, turning halfway through, until the chicken is cooked and shows no sign of pinkness inside.

Remove from the oven and sprinkle over the spring onion and extra dried chilli flakes, with slices of lime on the side.

The chicken will keep in the fridge for up to 2 days. To freeze, follow standard guidelines for defrosting and reheating.

AIR-FRYER METHOD
📷 **15 MINS** * PLUS 1 HOUR MARINATING

SPECIAL EQUIPMENT
Air fryer, 4 x wooden or metal skewers

In a bowl, combine the soy sauce, honey, sriracha sauce, chilli powder, tomato ketchup, garlic granules and chilli flakes. Add the chicken and stir to coat. Cover and pop into the fridge for an hour to marinate.

Preheat the air fryer to 180°C.

TIP:
If using wooden skewers, be sure to soak them in water for about 30 minutes before using. This will prevent them burning.

Once the chicken has marinated, thread the marinated meat evenly onto 4 skewers. Place the kebabs in the air-fryer basket and cook for 15 minutes, turning halfway through, until the chicken is cooked and shows no sign of pinkness inside.

Remove from the air fryer and sprinkle over the spring onion and extra dried chilli flakes, with slices of lime on the side.

The chicken will keep in the fridge for up to 2 days. To freeze, follow standard guidelines for defrosting and reheating.

CHICKEN PARMO

🕐 **15 MINS**　　🍲 **VARIABLE** (SEE BELOW)　　✕ **SERVES 2**

PER SERVING:
452 KCAL / 37G CARBS

2 skinless, boneless chicken
　breasts, about 150g each
1 tbsp cornflour
1 medium egg, beaten
50g panko breadcrumbs
low-calorie cooking spray
sea salt and freshly ground
　black pepper

FOR THE CHEESE SAUCE
1 tbsp plain flour
100ml skimmed milk
1 tsp Dijon mustard
¼ tsp paprika
30g reduced-fat spreadable
　cheese
20g reduced-fat mature
　Cheddar, finely grated

TO ACCOMPANY (OPTIONAL)
80g steamed vegetables
　(+ 38 kcal per serving) or 75g
　mixed salad (+ 15 kcal per
　serving)

This is our version of the ever-popular Teesside takeaway dish. Traditionally made from breaded chicken that's deep-fried and smothered in a calorie-laden béchamel sauce, our lighter version can be crisped up in the oven or air fryer. The slimming-friendly sauce is super quick to make in the microwave (yes, really!) using a combo of spreadable cheese and Cheddar to make it rich and creamy.

Weekly Indulgence ────────────────

OVEN METHOD
🍲 **35 MINS**

Preheat the oven to 220°C (fan 200°C/gas mark 7) and line a baking tray with a sheet of non-stick baking paper. Place a chicken breast between two sheets of non-stick baking paper and flatten with a rolling pin until it is about 2cm (¾in) thick. Place onto a plate and repeat with the other chicken breast.

Put the cornflour on a plate and season with salt and pepper. Place the beaten egg on second plate and the breadcrumbs on a third plate. Dip the flattened chicken breasts into the cornflour, coating both sides completely, then dip the floured chicken breasts into the beaten egg to coat completely. Now dip into the breadcrumbs to coat completely on both sides.

Place the breadcrumbed chicken breasts onto the lined baking tray and spray lightly with low-calorie cooking spray. Cook in the oven for 15 minutes, turn them over and spray again with low-calorie cooking spray. Cook for a further 15 minutes or until crisp, golden and the chicken shows no sign of pinkness inside.

You can freeze the breadcrumbed chicken breasts at this point. Layer between sheets of non-stick baking paper and store in a freezerproof container. Defrost overnight in the fridge then reheat in the air fryer or oven at 200°C until piping hot.

While the chicken is cooking, make the cheese sauce. Put the flour in a microwavable jug with 1 tablespoon of the milk. Stir to form a smooth paste. Add the rest of the milk and whisk until combined. Heat in 30-second blasts in the microwave, whisking after each blast until the mixture has thickened.

Continued...

Ours took 90 seconds, but this depends on the power of your microwave. Add the Dijon mustard, paprika, spreadable cheese and half of the Cheddar and whisk until melted and smooth. Season to taste with salt and pepper.

Once the chicken is cooked, spoon the cheese sauce over the top of each chicken breast. Sprinkle over the remaining cheese and pop under a preheated grill for 6 minutes, until the cheese is golden and bubbly.

Serve with your choice of accompaniment.

AIR-FRYER METHOD
🝪 **25 MINS**

SPECIAL EQUIPMENT
Air fryer

Place a chicken breast between two sheets of non-stick baking paper and flatten with a rolling pin until it is about 2cm (¾in) thick. Place onto a plate and repeat with the other chicken breast.

Put the cornflour on a plate and season with salt and pepper. Place the beaten egg on a second plate and the breadcrumbs on a third plate. Dip the flattened chicken breasts into the cornflour, turning to coat both sides completely, then dip the floured chicken breasts into the beaten egg to coat completely. Now dip them into the breadcrumbs to coat completely on both sides.

Preheat the air fryer to 200°C and line the base of the air-fryer basket with non-stick baking paper.

Place the breadcrumbed chicken breasts into the air-fryer basket and spray lightly with low-calorie cooking spray. Cook for 10 minutes, turn them over and spray again with low-calorie cooking spray. Cook for a further 10 minutes or until crisp, golden and the chicken shows no sign of pinkness inside.

You can freeze the breadcrumbed chicken breasts at this point, if you wish. Layer between sheets of non-stick baking paper and store in a freezerproof container. Defrost overnight in the fridge then reheat in the air fryer or oven at 200°C until piping hot.

While the chicken is cooking, make the cheese sauce. Put the flour in a microwavable jug with 1 tablespoon of the milk. Stir to form a smooth paste. Add the rest of the milk and whisk again until combined. Heat in 30-second blasts in the microwave, whisking after each blast until the mixture has thickened. Ours took 90 seconds, but this depends on the power of your microwave. Add the Dijon mustard, paprika, spreadable cheese and half of the Cheddar and whisk until melted and smooth. Season to taste with salt and pepper.

Once the chicken is cooked, spoon the cheese sauce over the top of each chicken breast. Sprinkle over the remaining cheese and pop back into the air fryer for 3–4 minutes, until the cheese is golden and bubbly.

Serve with your choice of accompaniment.

CRISPY GARLIC MUSHROOMS

🕐 **10 MINS** 🍲 **VARIABLE** (SEE BELOW) ✕ **SERVES 4**

PER SERVING:
144 KCAL / 14G CARBS

2 tsp cornflour
1 medium egg, beaten
1 garlic clove, peeled and crushed
150g button mushrooms (about 16 mushrooms)
low-calorie cooking spray

FOR THE CRISPY COATING
40g panko breadcrumbs
1 tsp garlic granules
¼ tsp salt
¼ tsp freshly ground black pepper

FOR THE DIP
4 tbsp reduced-fat mayonnaise
1 tsp finely chopped fresh chives

TO ACCOMPANY (OPTIONAL)
75g mixed salad (+ 15 kcal per serving)

These seriously crispy mushrooms are sure to make you feel like you're eating out! While they might have a crunch like they've been deep-fried, these beautiful baked bites are far lighter in calories than restaurant versions, without losing out on gloriously garlicky goodness. They're a must-try starter or side dish with our silky, chive-infused dip.

Everyday Light ─────────────────

OVEN METHOD
🍲 **20 MINS**

Preheat the oven to 220°C (fan 200°C/gas mark 7) and line a baking tray with a sheet of non-stick baking paper. Place the cornflour in a small bowl. Place the egg in a second small bowl and stir in the crushed garlic. In a third small bowl, add the breadcrumbs, garlic granules, salt and pepper, and stir.

Trim and discard the mushroom stalks. Add the mushrooms to the bowl of cornflour and toss to coat all over. Dip the floured mushrooms, one by one, into the egg mixture, then into the breadcrumb mixture, to coat all over. Place on the lined tray. Repeat until all the mushrooms are coated in breadcrumbs.

Spray the mushrooms with a little low-calorie cooking spray and bake in the oven for 20 minutes, until the mushrooms are tender, golden brown and crispy.

In a small bowl, combine the mayonnaise and chives. Serve as a dip with the mushrooms.

AIR-FRYER METHOD
🍲 **12 MINS**

SPECIAL EQUIPMENT
Air fryer

Place the cornflour in a small bowl. Place the egg in a second small bowl and stir in the crushed garlic. In a third small bowl, add the breadcrumbs, garlic granules, salt and pepper, and stir.

Trim and discard the mushroom stalks. Add the mushrooms to the bowl of cornflour and toss to coat all over.

Preheat the air fryer to 190°C. Dip the floured mushrooms, one by one, into the egg mixture, then into the breadcrumb mixture, to coat all over. Place onto a plate. Repeat until all the mushrooms are coated in breadcrumbs.

Place the mushrooms into the air-fryer basket and spray lightly with low-calorie cooking spray. Cook for 10–12 minutes, until the mushrooms are tender, golden brown and crispy.

In a small bowl, combine the mayonnaise and chives. Serve as a dip with the mushrooms.

VEGGIE

USE VEGETARIAN
BACON
ALTERNATIVE

**FREEZE
ME**

**BATCH
COOK**

**DAIRY
FREE**

USE DF CHEESE

**GLUTEN
FREE**

USE GF
BREADCRUMBS

MASHED POTATO BALLS

🕐 **15 MINS**   🍲 **VARIABLE** (SEE BELOW)   ✕ **SERVES 6**

PER SERVING:
166 KCAL /23G CARBS

500g potatoes, peeled and cut
    into chunks
low-calorie cooking spray
2 smoked bacon medallions
50g reduced-fat mature
    Cheddar, finely grated
2 spring onions, trimmed and
    very thinly sliced
6g fresh chives, very thinly sliced
½ tsp garlic granules
½ tsp onion powder
60g panko breadcrumbs
1 medium egg, beaten
sea salt and freshly ground
    black pepper

TO ACCOMPANY (OPTIONAL)
2 tbsp tomato ketchup (+ 15 kcal
    per tbsp)

Inspired by the loaded potato skins you often see on pub restaurant menus, these crispy balls of mashed potato have a fluffy cheese, onion and bacon filling. Coated in golden panko breadcrumbs, they're so easy and satisfying to make. You can crisp them up in the oven or in your air fryer and serve as a tasty snack or side dish.

Everyday Light —————————————————————

Preheat the oven to 200°C (fan 180°C /gas mark 6) and line a baking tray with non-stick baking paper.

Put the potatoes in a saucepan of cold water, place over a high heat and bring to the boil. Reduce the heat and simmer for 10–15 minutes, or until soft and cooked through. Drain well, mash and leave to cool.

While the potatoes are cooking, spray a small frying pan with low-calorie cooking spray and place over a medium heat. Add the bacon and fry for 2 minutes on each side or until cooked. Remove from the pan and dice finely.

Once the mash has cooled, add the bacon, cheese, spring onion, chives, garlic granules, onion powder and 20g of the panko breadcrumbs. Season to taste with salt and pepper and stir until evenly combined.

Take a little of the mixture and roll between your hands to create a 4cm (1½in) ball and place onto a plate. Repeat with the rest of the mixture – the mixture should make 24 balls.

Place the beaten egg on a plate and the remaining panko breadcrumbs on a second plate. Working one at a time, dip each ball into the egg, then into the breadcrumbs, getting an even coating all over. Place the coated balls onto the lined tray.

Once all the balls have been coated, spray with low-calorie cooking spray. Cook for 20–25 minutes until they are crisp and golden brown. The cooked balls will keep in the fridge for up to 3 days. To freeze, follow standard guidelines for defrosting and reheat in the oven at 200°C (fan 180°C /gas mark 6) until piping hot.

Continued...

AIR-FRYER METHOD
🍲 35 MINS

SPECIAL EQUIPMENT
Air fryer

Put the potatoes in a saucepan of cold water, place over a high heat and bring to the boil. Reduce the heat and simmer for 10–15 minutes, or until soft and cooked through. Drain well, mash and leave to cool.

While the potatoes are cooking, spray a small frying pan with low-calorie cooking spray and place over a medium heat. Add the bacon and fry for 2 minutes on each side or until cooked. Remove from the pan and dice finely.

Once the mash has cooled, add the bacon, cheese, spring onion, chives, garlic granules, onion powder and 20g of the panko breadcrumbs. Season to taste with salt and pepper and stir until evenly combined.

Preheat the air fryer to 170°C and line the base of the basket with non-stick baking paper.

Take a little of the potato mixture and roll between your hands to create a 4cm (1½in) ball and place onto a plate. Repeat with the rest of the mixture – the mixture should make 24 balls.

Place the beaten egg on a plate and the remaining panko breadcrumbs on a second plate. Working one at a time, dip each ball into the egg, then into the breadcrumbs, getting an even coating all over. Place the coated balls into the air-fryer basket.

Once all the balls have been coated, spray with low-calorie cooking spray. Cook for 15 minutes until they are crisp and golden brown.

The cooked balls will keep in the fridge for up to 3 days. To freeze, follow standard guidelines for defrosting and reheat in the air fryer at 170°C until piping hot.

TIP:
You may need to cook these in batches.

VEGGIE

FREEZE
ME

BATCH
COOK

GLUTEN
FREE

USE GF
FLOUR

MOCHA LAVA CAKES

🕐 **5 MINS**   🍲 **VARIABLE** (SEE BELOW)   ✕ **SERVES 4**

PER SERVING:
239 KCAL / 19G CARBS

SPECIAL EQUIPMENT
4 x 125ml ramekin dishes
or small cups

45g reduced-fat spread, plus
  a little extra for greasing
45g self-raising flour
25g white granulated sweetener
1 tbsp cocoa powder
2 medium eggs
1 tbsp espresso powder
20g milk chocolate (about
  4 squares)

FOR THE TOP
½ tsp icing sugar
½ tsp cocoa powder
5g milk chocolate (about
  1 square), chopped

Ready to pop in the oven (or microwave) after just 5 easy minutes of prep, these Mocha Lava Cakes hit the spot every time. They might be super quick and easy to make, but that doesn't make them any less impressive. We've added a hint of coffee to our chocolate sponge, and given each pud an irresistible, gooey chocolate centre. It's tough to believe they come in at less than 250 calories!

Weekly Indulgence ———————————————

OVEN METHOD
🍲 **10 MINS**

Preheat the oven to 180°C (fan 160°C/gas mark 4) and lightly grease the ramekin dishes with reduced-fat spread.

Place the self-raising flour, white granulated sweetener, cocoa powder, reduced-fat spread, eggs and espresso powder in a mixing bowl. Beat together for 1–2 minutes using an electric hand whisk or wooden spoon.

Divide the mixture evenly among the greased ramekin dishes and add one square of chocolate to the top of each. Place the ramekins onto a baking tray then bake in the oven for 8 minutes, until risen and spongy when pressed but still gooey in the middle.

Mix the icing sugar and cocoa powder together and dust the top of each lava cake. Sprinkle with the chopped chocolate and serve!

MICROWAVE METHOD
🍲 **4 MINS**

Lightly grease the ramekin dishes with reduced-fat spread.

Place the self-raising flour, white granulated sweetener, cocoa powder, reduced-fat spread, eggs and espresso powder in a mixing bowl. Beat together for 1–2 minutes using an electric hand whisk or wooden spoon.

Divide the mixture evenly among the greased ramekin dishes and add one square of chocolate to the top of each.

TIP:
Make sure to use white granulated sweetener that has the same weight, texture and sweetness as sugar, not powdered.

QUICK COOK

Cover each loosely with vented cling film (to allow steam to escape – they shouldn't be completely covered). Place into the microwave one at a time and cook on high for 1 minute. The cake should be risen but feel light to the touch. If the top is not cooked, place back in the microwave for 30 seconds (timing will depend on the power of your microwave). Remove the cling film.

Mix the icing sugar and cocoa powder together and dust the top of each lava cake. Sprinkle with the chopped chocolate and serve!

The cooked lava cakes can be frozen: wrap the ovenproof (and freezerproof) ramekins tightly in cling film, pack in a container and label. Defrost in the fridge. Cover loosely with vented cling film and microwave for about 30 seconds (see microwave method above), or reheat in a moderate oven for about 5 minutes.

TIP:

You could use instant coffee granules instead of espresso powder. Add to a food bag and bash with a rolling pin until you have a fine powder.

Quick
PREP

VEGGIE
USE VEGGIE SAUSAGES

DAIRY FREE

GLUTEN FREE
USE GF WRAPS AND SAUSAGES

BREAKFAST FOLDED WRAP

🕐 **10 MINS** 🗑 **25 MINS** ✕ **SERVES 2**

PER SERVING:
307 KCAL / 33G CARBS

low-calorie cooking spray
2 reduced-fat chicken chipolata
 sausages
4 mushrooms, sliced
2 low-calorie soft tortilla wraps,
 about 23cm / 9in diameter
200g baked beans in tomato
 sauce
2 medium eggs
2 cherry tomatoes, quartered
sea salt and freshly ground
 black pepper

Imagine your favourite full-English ingredients wrapped in a crispy, baked tortilla parcel... Don't be fooled by how simple this ingredients list is – the flavours really deliver! We've folded sausage, beans, egg, mushrooms and tomatoes into ours, but you could get creative with different fillings.

Everyday Light ───────────────────

Preheat the oven to 210°C (fan 190°C/gas mark 6) and line a baking tray with non-stick baking paper.

Spray a frying pan with low-calorie cooking spray and place over a medium heat. Add the sausages and fry for 3 minutes, then add the mushrooms and fry for a further 3 minutes. The sausages should be browned on all sides and the mushrooms softened. Remove the sausages from the pan, cut into 8 slices each and leave to one side.

Microwave the tortilla wraps for 30 seconds; this will make them easier to fold. Lay a wrap on the work surface. Fold the sides in towards the centre, leaving a gap of roughly 6cm (2½in). Fold the top and bottom sides of the wrap in towards the centre (there should now be a long, rectangular window in the centre of the wrap). Press the folds well.

Unfold the wrap and you should be able to see the fold lines. Spread half the beans into the square in the centre of the wrap. Once spread out, make a small circle shape in the beans by pushing the beans aside (creating a border of beans to hold the egg later). Add half the mushrooms on top of the beans, then 8 of the sausage slices. Brush the exposed edges of the wrap with a little cold water. Crack an egg into the centre of the beans. Refold the wrap, starting with the sides, then fold in the top and bottom. Add a little more water on the overlapping corners and press the edges together so that the filling is sealed well inside the folded wrap.

Nestle 4 tomato quarters on top of the egg and season with salt and pepper. Transfer to the lined baking tray and repeat with the second wrap. Spray the top of the wraps with a little low-calorie cooking spray and pop the tray into the oven for 20 minutes. The egg white should be set, and the wrap should be turning golden brown. Remove from the oven and serve.

TIP:
Want to make it vegetarian? Simply swap out the chipolatas for meat-free sausages!

QUICK PREP

VEGGIE

FREEZE ME

BATCH COOK

BANANA AND BLUEBERRY MUFFINS

🕐 **10 MINS**   🗑 **25 MINS**   ✕ **MAKES 12**

PER SERVING:
188 KCAL /30G CARBS

SPECIAL EQUIPMENT
12-hole muffin tin, 12 paper muffin cases, electric whisk (useful but not essential)

80g reduced-fat spread, softened slightly
80g fat-free Greek yoghurt
80g white granulated sweetener
2 medium bananas, peeled and mashed with a fork
2 medium eggs, beaten
300g self-raising flour
60g fresh blueberries
15g milk chocolate chips

We love a muffin for breakfast, but shop-bought versions can be surprisingly high in calories. Batch cook these Banana and Blueberry Muffins for a grab-and-go brekkie that's just as convenient (and even more delicious) on a busy day. At just 188 calories each, they even include a little sprinkle of chocolate chips. We always make extra so we can stock up the freezer – just leave a couple to defrost overnight and that's breakfast sorted!

Everyday Light

Preheat the oven to 200°C (fan 180°C/gas mark 6). Place 12 paper muffin cases into the 12-hole muffin tin and leave to one side.

Place the reduced-fat spread, yoghurt and granulated sweetener into a mixing bowl. Mix with an electric whisk for 1 minute, until smooth. Alternatively, you can use a wooden spoon, but this will take more effort. Add the mashed bananas and mix until combined, then add the eggs and beat until smooth. Add the flour and mix again until the mixture just comes together into a smooth batter. Avoid over-mixing as this can result in a tough muffin once baked.

Divide the mixture equally among the muffin cases. Top each with a few of the blueberries and chocolate chips. Lightly press the blueberries and chocolate chips into the surface of the mixture.

Bake in the oven for 25 minutes, until the tops of the muffins are lightly golden, and a skewer inserted into the middle of the muffins comes out clean. Leave to cool completely.

The muffins will keep in the fridge for up to 3 days. To freeze, follow standard guidelines for defrosting and reheating.

TIP:
Make sure to use white granulated sweetener that has the same weight, texture and sweetness as sugar.

QUICK PREP

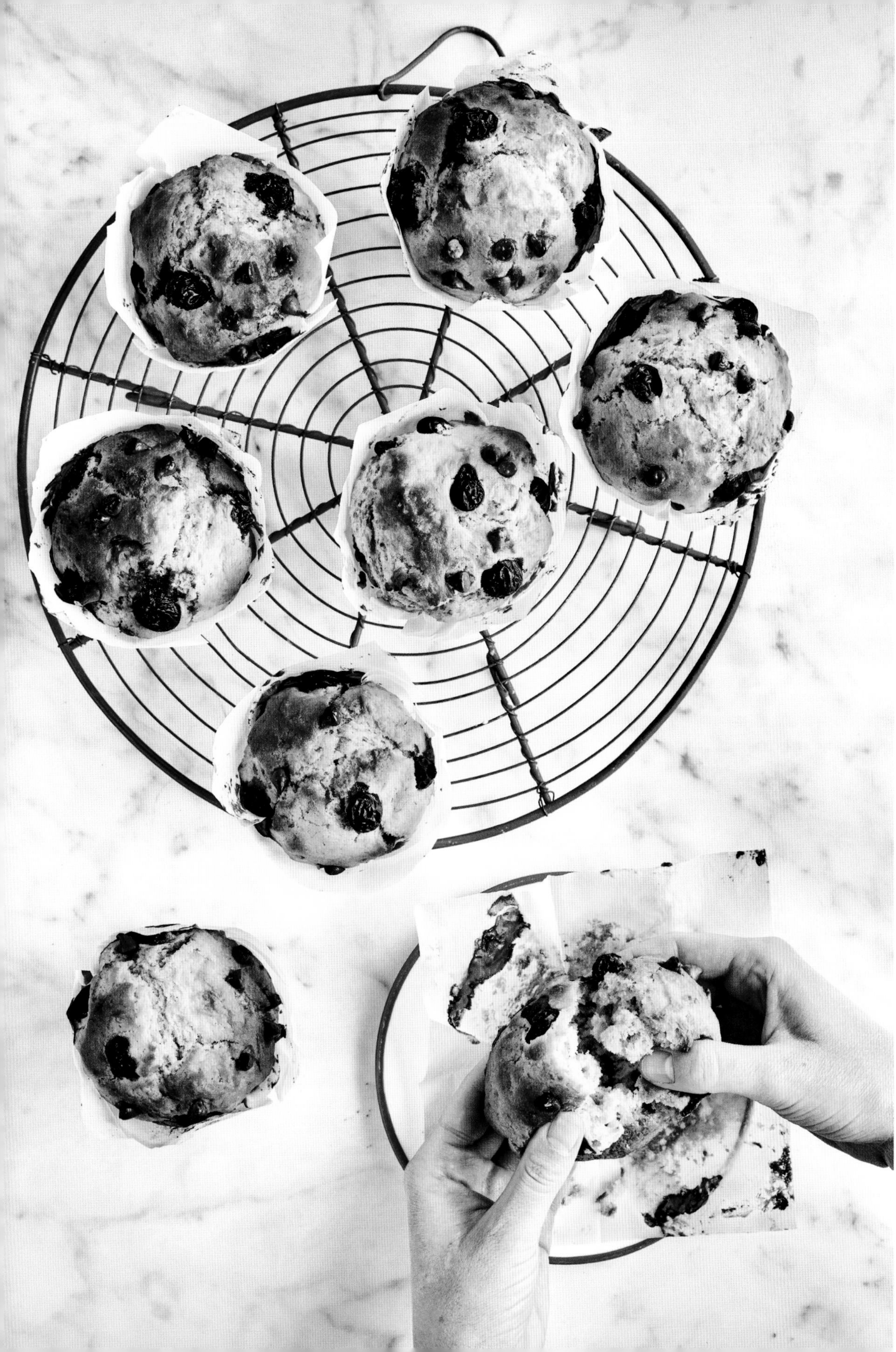

EGG AND BACON PIES

⏱ **15 MINS**   🍲 **35 MINS**   ✕ **MAKES 6**

PER PIE:
165 KCAL /12G CARBS

SPECIAL EQUIPMENT
Deep muffin tin (holes 6cm/2½in diameter and 3.5cm/1½in deep)

low-calorie cooking spray
1 medium onion, peeled and finely chopped
2 smoked bacon medallions, cut into small dice
12 x 12cm (5 x 5in) filo pastry squares
6 medium eggs, plus 1 medium egg, beaten, for glazing
1 spring onion, trimmed and finely chopped
sea salt and freshly ground black pepper

TO ACCOMPANY (OPTIONAL)
¼ tin reduced-sugar baked beans (+ 85 kcal per serving)

Any recipe that involves eggs and bacon is always a winner, but we think we've improved on perfection by baking them inside our golden filo pastry cases. For breakfast, lunch or a mid-afternoon snack, these savoury little pies are a game changer. They're really simple to make – and hot or cold, the crisp, light filo brings such a satisfying crunch.

Everyday Light ———————————————

Preheat the oven to 180°C (fan 160°C/gas mark 4).

Spray a small frying pan with low-calorie cooking spray and place over a medium heat. Add the onion and fry gently for 5–10 minutes until softened, then add the bacon and cook for a further 4–5 minutes until the bacon is cooked and the onion is soft and golden. Season with pepper and set aside.

Spray 6 of the muffin tin holes with low-calorie cooking spray and use to grease thoroughly. Take one filo pastry square and brush one side with beaten egg. Carefully press the filo square down into a muffin tin hole, glazed side up, to form a pastry case. Repeat with a second square of pastry, placing it at an angle to the first and glazed side up. The pastry case should have fluted, curled sides that stick up above the rim of the muffin tin (the pastry cases need to be deep enough to fit a whole egg in). Repeat this process until you have made 6 pastry cases.

Place the muffin tin in the preheated oven and bake the pastry cases for 2–3 minutes, until partly baked. The egg glaze will have just dried out and the pastry will still be mostly white, turning light golden in places. Remove from the oven and leave the pastry cases in the muffin tin.

Divide the onion and bacon mixture between the 6 part-baked pastry cases. Crack a whole egg into each pastry case. Season the top of the eggs with salt and pepper, sprinkle the tops with chopped spring onion and bake in the oven for 15–20 minutes, until the eggs are set and cooked through. Watch carefully as the pastry cases can burn easily.

Serve hot or cold with baked beans if you wish.

TIP:
Use a deep muffin tin rather than a shallow bun tin so there will be enough room for the whole eggs to fit in.

SWEET AND SOUR HALLOUMI CURRY

🕐 **15 MINS**　　🍲 **55 MINS**　　✕ **SERVES 4**

PER SERVING:
329 KCAL / 30G CARBS

low-calorie cooking spray
1 medium onion, peeled and diced
1 pepper (any colour), deseeded and diced
4 garlic cloves, peeled and crushed
2.5cm (1in) piece of root ginger, peeled and finely grated
1 tbsp garam masala
½–1 tsp dried chilli flakes, depending how hot you like it
1 tsp fenugreek seeds
1 tbsp tamarind paste
1 x 400g tin chopped tomatoes
700ml vegetable stock (1 vegetable stock cube dissolved in 700ml boiling water)
75g dried red split lentils
225g reduced-fat halloumi, cut into 1.5cm (¾in) cubes
250g cauliflower, broken into bite-sized florets
100g fresh pineapple, peeled and cut into small cubes
handful of fresh coriander leaves, chopped

TO ACCOMPANY
1 roti per portion (+ 167 kcal per roti)

You might be thinking halloumi in a curry sounds a little strange, but don't knock it till you try it! The salty flavour and chewy texture is perfect for this dhansak-inspired fakeaway. Similar to one of our favourite takeaway curries, this vegetarian recipe gets a sour tang from tamarind paste and a pop of sweetness from fresh pineapple. Just wait until you taste all those vibrant flavours in every delicious, slimming-friendly forkful.

Weekly Indulgence ————————————————

Preheat the oven to 220°C (fan 200°C/gas mark 7).

Spray a large frying pan or wok with low-calorie cooking spray and place over a medium heat. Add the onion and pepper and fry for 8–10 minutes until the onion is soft and golden, then add the garlic, ginger, garam masala, chilli flakes and fenugreek seeds and fry for another minute or two, until fragrant. Add the tamarind paste, tomatoes and stock and stir in the lentils. Bring to the boil, then reduce the heat to a simmer, cover and cook for 25 minutes.

While the sauce cooks, spread the halloumi cubes and cauliflower florets onto a baking sheet, spray with low-calorie cooking spray and cook in the oven for 15 minutes, until golden.

After 25 minutes, check the sauce. If it is too thick, you can add a little more water at this point, until you have a consistency you like.

Stir the cauliflower, halloumi and pineapple into the sauce, replace the lid and cook for a further 10 minutes. Don't stir too much as you don't want the halloumi to break up.

Stir in the coriander and serve with rotis.

The curry will keep in the fridge for up to 3 days. To freeze, follow standard guidelines for defrosting and reheating.

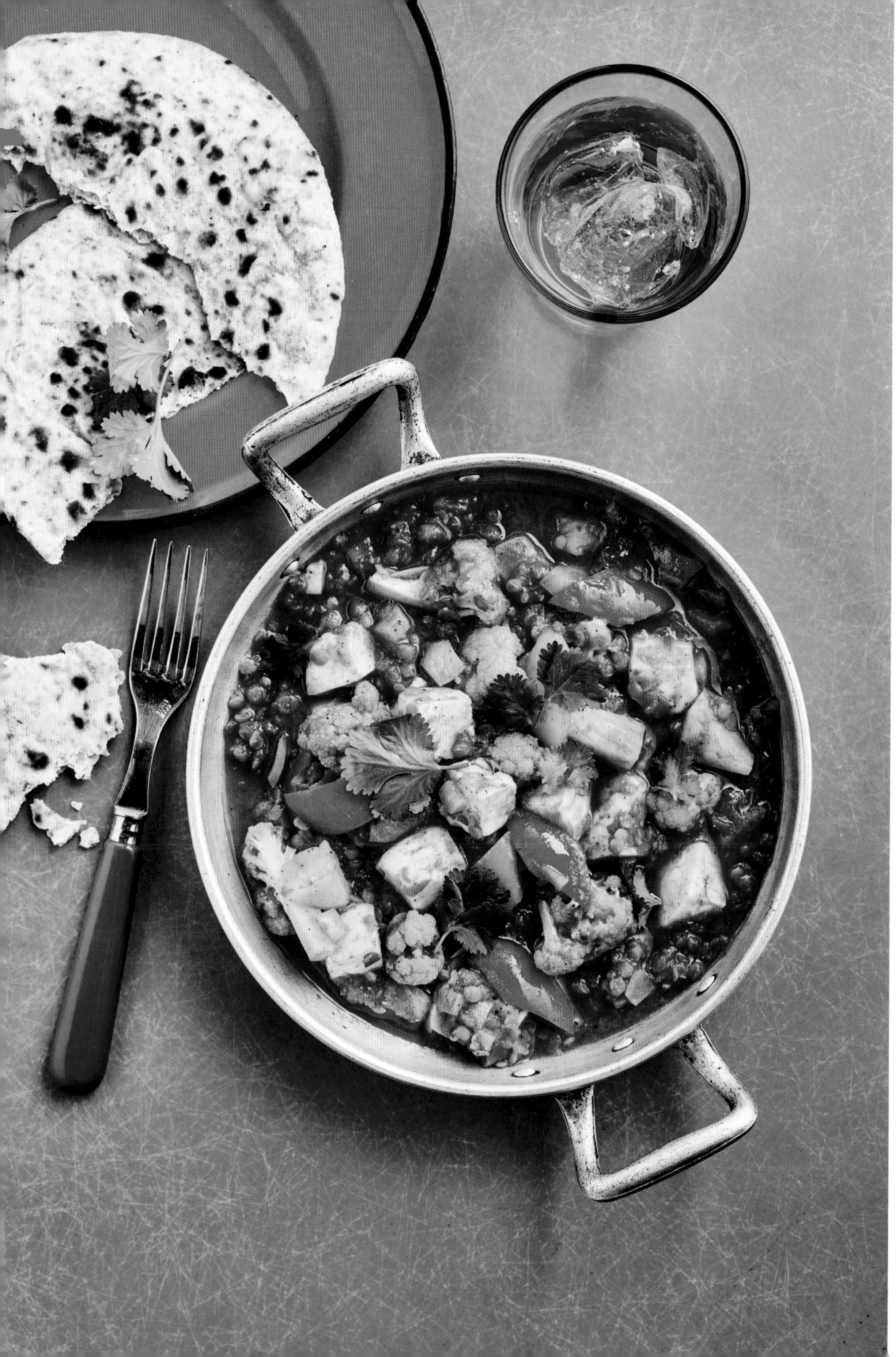

TOFU AND COCONUT CURRY

🕐 **15 MINS**   🍲 **30 MINS**   ✕ **SERVES 4**

* PLUS 30 MINUTES PRESSING

VEGGIE

VEGAN

FREEZE ME

BATCH COOK

DAIRY FREE

GLUTEN FREE

USE GF STOCK CUBE

PER SERVING:
285 KCAL /18G CARBS

300g block of firm tofu
low-calorie cooking spray
1 tbsp cornflour
1 red pepper, deseeded and sliced
1 onion, peeled and diced
2 garlic cloves, peeled and crushed
2cm (¾in) piece of root ginger, peeled and finely grated
2 tbsp tomato puree
1 tbsp curry powder
250ml vegetable stock (1 vegetable stock cube dissolved in 250ml boiling water)
1 x 400g tin light coconut milk
150g baby corn, each cut into thirds
150g sugar snap peas
1 lime, half juiced, the other half cut into wedges for garnish
sea salt and freshly ground black pepper
handful of fresh coriander leaves, roughly chopped, to serve

TO ACCOMPANY
50g uncooked basmati rice per portion, cooked according to packet instructions (+ 173 kcal per 125g cooked serving)

TIP:

Tofu comes in different varieties. The best variety for this recipe is firm or extra firm (silken tofu is not suitable).

Imagine oven-baked tofu, red pepper, baby corn and sugar snap peas, all cooked in a creamy, dairy-free coconut-based curry sauce. This easy, speedy, vegan curry has bags of flavour, for so few calories. You'll want to make sure you pick up some firm tofu for this recipe, so that it holds its shape and gives a nice bite to the finished curry.

Weekly Indulgence ────────────────

Remove the tofu from its packaging and drain. Wrap in a clean tea towel and place on a plate. Place a heavy pan on top and leave for 30 minutes. Pressing the tofu like this gets rid of excess liquid and produces a better texture.

Preheat the oven to 220°C (fan 200°C/gas mark 7).

Cut the pressed tofu into 2cm (¾in) chunks and place in a bowl. Spritz with low-calorie cooking spray then sprinkle the cornflour over and season well with salt and pepper. Toss to evenly coat the tofu.

Spray a non-stick baking tray with low-calorie cooking spray and scatter the tofu over. Spray the tofu with low-calorie cooking spray and cook in the oven for 15 minutes, until golden and crisp. Meanwhile, prepare the curry.

Spray a large frying pan or wok with low-calorie cooking spray and place over a medium heat. Add the pepper and onion and sauté for 5 minutes until soft, then add the garlic and ginger and cook for another minute. Stir in the tomato puree and curry powder. Add the stock, coconut milk and oven-baked tofu, bring to the boil then reduce the heat and simmer uncovered for 10 minutes.

Add the baby corn, sugar snap peas and lime juice. Cook for a further 10 minutes, until the vegetables are cooked and the sauce has thickened. You can adjust the consistency of the sauce: if you feel it is too runny, turn up the heat and simmer rapidly for a couple of minutes. If it seems too thick add a splash of water.

Stir in the chopped coriander and serve with rice, garnished with lime wedges.

FAKEAWAYS

LOADED PUPPY FRIES

🕐 **15 MINS**　　🍲 **25 MINS**　　✕ **SERVES 4**

PER SERVING:
381 KCAL / 44G CARBS

1 tsp smoked paprika
½ tsp hot chilli powder
½ tsp ground coriander
½ tsp garlic granules
½ tsp onion powder
800g potatoes, peeled
6 chicken chipolatas (about
　200g), sliced into bite-sized
　sections
low-calorie cooking spray

FOR THE COLESLAW

2 tbsp reduced-fat mayonnaise
2 tbsp cider vinegar
½ tsp sriracha sauce
100g white cabbage, thinly
　sliced
1 medium carrot, peeled and
　coarsely grated
sea salt and freshly ground
　black pepper

FOR THE SALSA ROSADA SAUCE

2 tbsp reduced-fat mayonnaise
1 tbsp tomato ketchup
a few splashes of
　Worcestershire sauce or
　Henderson's relish
½ tsp garlic granules

FOR THE TOP

60g reduced-fat Cheddar, finely
　grated

These unmissable loaded fries are inspired by the popular street food, Venezuelan hot dogs. We've made some skinny-cut chips and baked them with chicken sausages, coated in a blend of herbs and spices. Serve drizzled with our Salsa Rosada sauce, which is made from mayonnaise and ketchup with a dash of Worcestershire sauce, and don't forget to spoon on the crunchy coleslaw. We guarantee empty plates all round!

Everyday Light ─────────────────

Preheat the oven to 210°C (fan 190°C/gas mark 6). In a small bowl, combine the paprika, chilli powder, coriander, garlic granules and onion powder.

Cut the potatoes into fine chips, about 5mm (¼in) in width, then put them on a baking tray along with the sliced chipolatas. Spray with low-calorie cooking spray, sprinkle the spice mix over the chips and chipolatas and toss to coat. Pop into the oven for 25 minutes or until the fries are golden and crisp and the sausages are cooked.

While the chips and chipolatas are cooking, make the coleslaw. In a bowl combine the mayonnaise, cider vinegar, sriracha and some salt and pepper and stir until smooth. Add the cabbage and carrot and coat in the mayonnaise mixture. Leave to one side.

To make the sauce, mix the mayonnaise, ketchup, Worcestershire sauce or Henderson's relish and garlic granules in a small bowl until smooth.

When the fries are golden brown and crispy and the chipolatas cooked through, remove from the oven and add to your serving plates. Sprinkle over the cheese and add a drizzle of the sauce. Serve with a scoop of coleslaw.

USE GF CURRY PASTE

FRAGRANT CHICKEN CURRY

🕐 **5 MINS**   🍲 **30 MINS**   ✕ **SERVES 4**

PER SERVING:
321 KCAL /21G CARBS

low-calorie cooking spray
8 shallots, peeled and diced
1 red pepper, deseeded and
    diced
420g diced chicken breast
170g potatoes, peeled and diced
1 carrot, peeled and thinly sliced
1 x 185g jar of Malaysian curry
    paste
300ml coconut plant-based
    drink
1 tsp white granulated
    sweetener
1 tsp cornflour
fresh coriander leaves to serve
    (optional)

TO ACCOMPANY
50g uncooked basmati rice per
    portion, cooked according to
    packet instructions (+ 173 kcal
    per 125g cooked serving)

We're all for a budget-friendly, time-saving hack, so this recipe uses a shop-bought Malaysian curry paste to save on buying a long list of ingredients. Mild and aromatic, our Fragrant Chicken Curry gets its creaminess from a coconut plant-based drink, which also keeps it lower in calories. It's on the table in just 35 minutes and, best of all, you'll only have one pan to wash up after dinner!

Weekly Indulgence ────────────────

Spray a large frying pan with low-calorie cooking spray and place over a medium heat. Add the shallots and pepper and fry for 3 minutes, until starting to soften. Add the chicken and cook for 4–5 minutes or until browned on all sides, then add the potatoes, carrot and curry paste and stir to coat the chicken and vegetables.

Pour in the coconut drink and add the sweetener. Bring to the boil then turn down the heat to low, cover with a lid and simmer for 20 minutes.

Mix the cornflour and 1 teaspoon of cold water in a small bowl until combined. Pour into the curry. The curry should thicken slightly but still have a broth-like consistency. Serve with rice, scattered with fresh coriander leaves if you like.

The curry will keep in the fridge for up to 3 days. To freeze, follow standard guidelines for defrosting and reheating.

VEGGIE

SWAP CHICKEN FOR QUORN AND USE A VEGETABLE STOCK CUBE

FREEZE ME

BATCH COOK

DAIRY FREE

GLUTEN FREE

USE GF STOCK CUBE AND SOY SAUCE

LEMON AND GINGER CHICKEN

 10 MINS   **20 MINS**   **SERVES 4**

PER SERVING:
233 KCAL /19G CARBS

low-calorie cooking spray
500g diced chicken breast
1 medium onion, peeled and sliced
5cm (2in) piece of root ginger (about 20g), peeled and finely grated
2 garlic cloves, peeled and crushed
juice of 2 large lemons
1½ tbsp light soy sauce
2 tbsp honey
400ml chicken stock (1 chicken stock cube dissolved in 400ml boiling water)
1 tbsp cornflour
150g sugar snap peas
lemon slices, to serve (optional)

TO ACCOMPANY

50g uncooked basmati rice per portion, cooked according to packet instructions (+ 173 kcal per 125g cooked serving)

Everybody loves an easy-peasy Friday night fakeaway! Inspired by sweet yet tangy takeaway flavours, we've cooked our chicken in a punchy homemade lemon and ginger sauce. Ready in 30 minutes, and only 233 calories per portion, there's no excuse not to give it a try. While we think rice works best to soak up every drop of sauce, the citrus and ginger flavours pair nicely with noodles too.

Weekly Indulgence ─────────────────────

Spray a wok or large frying pan with low-calorie cooking spray and place over a medium-high heat. When hot, add the chicken and stir-fry for 5 minutes until browned. Remove from the pan and set to one side.

Spray the wok or pan with a little more low-calorie cooking spray and add the onion. Fry for about 4 minutes, until beginning to soften, then add the ginger and garlic and cook for a further minute. Add the lemon juice, soy sauce, honey and stock, stir and bring to the boil.

Mix the cornflour and 1 tablespoon of cold water in a small bowl until combined, then quickly stir it into the sauce and simmer for a few minutes until the sauce has thickened.

Return the chicken to the pan, along with the sugar snap peas, and simmer for 5–8 minutes, until the chicken is cooked through and shows no sign of pinkness inside.

Serve with basmati rice and garnished with lemon slices, if you like.

The chicken will keep in the fridge for up to 3 days. To freeze, follow standard guidelines for defrosting and reheating.

QUICK PREP

TIP:
We've added a pop of green with sugar snap peas, but any crunchy stir-fried veg will do.

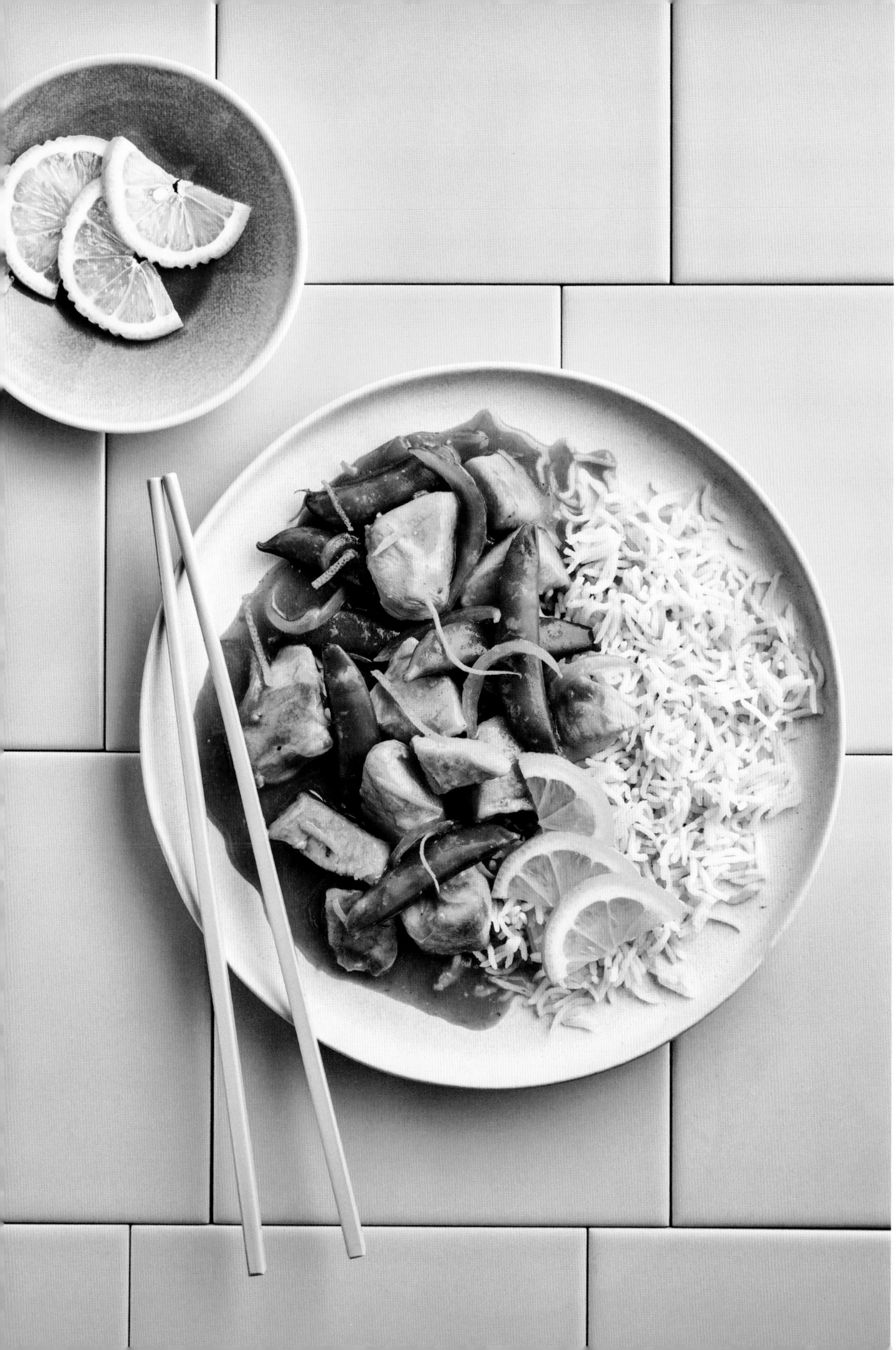

PERI-PERI PULLED CHICKEN WRAPS

🕐 **15 MINS**　　🍲 **20 MINS**　　✗ **SERVES 4**

FREEZE ME

CHICKEN FILLING ONLY

DAIRY FREE

USE DF MAYONNAISE

GLUTEN FREE

USE GF WRAPS

PER SERVING:
267 KCAL / 30G CARBS

FOR THE PERI-PERI CHICKEN FILLING

2 skinless, boneless chicken breasts (visible fat removed), about 260g in total
low-calorie cooking spray
1 medium red pepper, deseeded and thinly sliced
2 garlic cloves, peeled and crushed
2 tsp peri-peri seasoning
½ tsp sweet smoked paprika
½ tsp onion powder
½ tsp mild chilli powder
250g passata

TO SERVE

4 low-calorie soft tortilla wraps
2 tbsp reduced-fat mayonnaise
1 tsp honey
¼ tsp sriracha sauce
100g iceberg lettuce, thinly sliced
50g cucumber, finely diced

You can't say no to these crunchy Chicken Wraps, especially if you're already peri-peri obsessed! To bring you your favourite restaurant flavours in the comfort of your own home, we've pan-fried the shredded chicken in a herby, medium-spiced peri-peri sauce. Roll it into a low-calorie tortilla wrap with fresh lettuce, cucumber and homemade spicy mayo for a delicious light lunch (they're only 267 calories each!).

Everyday Light

Put the chicken breasts in a medium saucepan and pour over cold water until just covered. Place over a medium heat and bring to the boil, lower the heat and simmer gently for 12 minutes. Check that the chicken is cooked through, and no pinkness remains.

While the chicken is cooking, spray a large frying pan with low-calorie cooking spray and place over a low heat. Add the red pepper and fry for 5 minutes, then add the garlic and fry for a further 3 minutes. Sprinkle over the peri-peri seasoning, paprika, onion powder and chilli powder. Fry for 1 minute until the spices become fragrant then pour in the passata. Simmer gently for 4 minutes.

Once the chicken is cooked, remove from the saucepan to a plate and shred the meat with two forks. Add to the frying pan and continue to simmer for 5 minutes, until the passata has reduced and the chicken is coated in the sauce. You can chill or freeze the chicken and sauce at this point, if you like. It will keep in the fridge for up to 3 days. To freeze, follow standard guidelines for defrosting and reheating.

Heat the tortilla wraps according to the packet instructions. We did this in the microwave for 60 seconds.

In a small bowl, combine the mayonnaise, honey and sriracha sauce until smooth.

Lay a tortilla wrap flat onto the surface and spread a little of the spicy mayonnaise on the bottom section of the wrap. Add some of the peri-peri chicken filling, lettuce and cucumber.

FAKEAWAYS

FREEZE ME

BATCH COOK

GLUTEN FREE

USE GF STOCK CUBE

CREAMY CHIPOTLE BEEF

🕐 **10 MINS**　　🍲 **20 MINS**　　✕ **SERVES 4**

PER SERVING:
245 KCAL /10G CARBS

low-calorie cooking spray
500g quick-cook steak, cut
　into thin strips (e.g., rump,
　medallions, sirloin)
2 peppers (any colour),
　deseeded and sliced
1 onion, peeled and thinly sliced
2 garlic cloves, peeled and
　crushed
1 tbsp tomato puree
4 tsp chipotle paste
300ml beef stock (1 beef stock
　cube dissolved in 300ml boiling
　water)
75g reduced-fat cream cheese
juice of ½ lime, plus wedges to
　garnish
handful of fresh coriander
　leaves, chopped

TO ACCOMPANY
50g uncooked basmati rice per
　portion, cooked according to
　packet instructions (+ 173 kcal
　per 125g cooked serving)

This is your cue to grab your wok! Our Creamy Chipotle Beef needs to be on your midweek menu. We wanted this stir-fry to feel extra special without piling on the calories, so we've added a touch of luxury to our beef strips using reduced-fat cream cheese. Sweet, smoky and silky, try this chilli stir-fry with a difference alongside rice, potatoes or a crunchy corn on the cob.

Weekly Indulgence ──────────────────

Spray a large frying pan or wok with low-calorie cooking spray and place over a medium-high heat. When the pan is hot, add the beef strips and stir-fry for 3–4 minutes until cooked. Remove from the pan and put to one side.

Give the pan another spray of low-calorie cooking spray, if needed, then add the peppers and onion and stir-fry for 5 minutes until the vegetables begin to soften. Add the garlic, tomato puree and chipotle paste and cook for a further minute, then add the stock. Bring to a simmer then stir in the cream cheese until completely blended. Simmer for 6–7 minutes, until the sauce is the consistency of single cream.

Add the steak back to the pan and cook for 2–3 minutes, until heated through.

Stir in the lime juice, sprinkle over the coriander and serve with rice and lime wedges on the side.

This dish can be kept in the fridge for up to 2 days. To freeze, follow standard guidelines for defrosting and reheating.

VEGGIE

VEGAN

USE QUORN

DAIRY FREE

CHECK CHICKEN SEASONING LABEL

GLUTEN FREE

USE GF SOY SAUCE

SHREDDED VEGETABLE AND CHICKEN SALAD

🕐 **15 MINS**   🍲 **25 MINS**   ✕ **SERVES 4**

PER SERVING:
187 KCAL /11G CARBS

FOR THE SALAD
2 skinless, boneless chicken breasts (175g each)
1 tsp chicken seasoning
100g frozen edamame beans
80g kale, finely shredded
80g sweetheart cabbage, finely shredded
80g red cabbage, finely shredded
1 carrot, peeled and julienned or grated
2 spring onions, trimmed and thinly sliced

FOR THE DRESSING
2 tbsp lime juice
2 tbsp sweet chilli sauce
1 tsp soy sauce
1 tsp Chinese rice wine
¼ tsp peanut butter powder
½ red chilli, deseeded and finely diced
2g fresh coriander leaves, finely chopped

This simple salad is so satisfying! The finely shredded veggies are drizzled in a mildly spicy dressing, with a tang of sweet chilli and a hint of peanut butter flavour. With carrot, red cabbage, kale and edamame beans in the mix, you'll feel like you're eating the rainbow with every bite. This quick recipe is ready to eat in just 40 minutes, but you can save on preparation time if you have a food processor to speed up slicing the vegetables!

Everyday Light ————————————————

Preheat the oven to 210°C (fan 190°C/gas mark 6).

Place the chicken breasts on a baking tray and sprinkle over the chicken seasoning. Cook in the oven for 25 minutes, or until the chicken is cooked through: the juices should run clear and no pinkness remain.

Add the edamame beans to a small saucepan, cover with boiling water and cook according to the packet instructions. Tip into a colander, then under cold running water, then drain.

Add the dressing ingredients to a small bowl and mix until no lumps of peanut butter powder remain.

Add the kale, sweetheart cabbage, red cabbage and carrot to a large bowl and toss to combine. Divide between four serving plates. Add the edamame beans and spring onions to the top of the salad.

Once the chicken is cooked, slice and arrange on top of each plate of salad.

Drizzle over the dressing and serve.

TIPS:
Try to slice the vegetables and kale very finely to get a rainbow mix in every bite!
You could substitute Chinese rice wine with dry sherry or mirin.

QUICK PREP

VEGGIE
USE VEGGIE SAUSAGES

FREEZE ME

BATCH COOK

GLUTEN FREE
USE GF PASTA AND SAUSAGES

SAUSAGE AND TOMATO MAC 'N' CHEESE

🕐 **10 MINS**   🍲 **40 MINS**   ✕ **SERVES 4**

PER SERVING:
482 KCAL / 58G CARBS

SPECIAL EQUIPMENT
**Large ovenproof dish
(about 18 x 27cm/7 x 10½in)**

low-calorie cooking spray
4 reduced-fat pork sausages
200g cherry tomatoes, halved
1 tsp dried sage
½ tsp garlic granules
200g dried macaroni
500ml skimmed milk
25g reduced-fat spread
3 tbsp cornflour
120g reduced-fat mature
  Cheddar, finely grated
¼ tsp mustard powder
sea salt and freshly ground
  black pepper

TO ACCOMPANY (OPTIONAL)
75g mixed salad (+ 15 kcal per
  serving)

TIP:
Try using different
small pasta shapes,
such as penne.

Who can say no to Mac 'n' Cheese? This twist on everyone's favourite comfort food adds meaty flavour from reduced-fat sausages and an intense pop of sweetness from roasted tomatoes. We've kept things slimming friendly by making our own cheese sauce, using skimmed milk and reduced-fat cheese. This one's going to be a hit with the whole family!

Weekly Indulgence

Preheat the oven to 220°C (fan 200°C/gas mark 7) and spray the ovenproof dish with low-calorie cooking spray.

Place the sausages in the ovenproof dish and add the tomatoes, cut side up. Sprinkle over the sage and garlic granules, spray with low-calorie cooking spray and cook in the oven for 20 minutes, turning the sausages halfway through, or until the sausages are cooked, show no signs of pinkness and are golden brown. The tomatoes should be wrinkling around the edges.

Remove the sausages and tomatoes from the oven and cut the sausages into quarters. Set aside.

Meanwhile, put the macaroni in a large saucepan of boiling water, then lower the heat and partially cover with a lid. Simmer for about 10 minutes or until al dente. It will be ready when the pasta is tender when you bite a piece, but not too soft. Drain and return to the pan, putting the lid on to keep it warm. Set aside, off the heat.

Place the milk in a small saucepan, add the reduced-fat spread, and heat gently until steaming hot and the reduced-fat spread has melted. Take care not to let the milk boil over.

Put the cornflour in a bowl with 3 tablespoons of cold water and mix until smooth. Pour into the hot milk, stirring constantly with a balloon whisk or wooden spoon. Simmer for 3–5 minutes, stirring constantly, until thickened slightly and smooth. Stir in 100g of the grated cheese and the mustard powder.

Place the sausage quarters, roasted tomatoes (save a few or the top) and cheese sauce in the saucepan with the drained macaroni and stir to combine. Season to taste with salt and pepper.

QUICK PREP

Wash the ovenproof dish then add the macaroni, sausage and tomato mixture and spread it out. Sprinkle the top with the remaining 20g of grated Cheddar and place the rest of the roasted tomatoes on top.

Bake in the oven for 15–20 minutes, or until bubbling and golden. Serve with a mixed salad or other accompaniment of your choice.

The dish will keep in the fridge for 1–2 days. To freeze, follow standard guidelines for defrosting and reheating.

SALT AND PEPPER CHICKEN SALAD

⏱ **15 MINS**   🍲 **30 MINS**   ✕ **SERVES 4**

PER SERVING:
354 KCAL /40G CARBS

1 tbsp fine sea salt
1 tbsp white granulated sweetener or caster sugar
½ tbsp Chinese 5 spice
pinch of dried chilli flakes
1 tsp ground white pepper
75g panko breadcrumbs
1 medium egg, beaten
400g diced chicken breast
low-calorie cooking spray
300g Chinese leaves, thinly sliced
150g chilled, cooked edamame beans
50g fresh beansprouts
½ medium red pepper, deseeded and finely diced
½ medium green pepper, deseeded and finely diced
2 spring onions, trimmed and finely chopped
1 small red chilli, deseeded and finely chopped (optional)
8 tbsp readymade reduced-sugar sweet chilli sauce
lime slices, to serve (optional)

Nothing has us looking forward to lunchtime quite like this fakeaway-inspired crispy chicken salad. It's every bit as fun and delicious as it sounds, for only 313 calories per serving (drizzle of sweet chilli sauce included!). We think it really shines on a bed of Asian-style veggies, but there's nothing to stop you swapping in your favourite shredded greens – just be sure to tweak the calories, if you're counting!

Everyday Light

Preheat the oven to 200°C (fan 180°C/gas mark 6) and line a large baking tray with a sheet of non-stick baking paper.

Place a small frying pan over a low heat, add the sea salt and toast for 1–2 minutes until lightly golden.

Place the toasted sea salt in a small bowl with the sweetener or sugar, Chinese 5 spice, chilli flakes, white pepper and panko breadcrumbs and mix well.

Place the beaten egg on a plate and the salt-and-pepper breadcrumbs on another plate. Dip the chicken pieces in the egg to coat all over, then dip in the salt-and-pepper breadcrumbs to coat completely.

Place the chicken nuggets on the lined baking tray, leaving space between each and spray with low-calorie cooking spray. Bake in the preheated oven for 25–30 minutes, turning the chicken pieces halfway through, until crisp and golden. Make sure the chicken shows no sign of pinkness and the juices run clear.

Divide the Chinese leaves among plates and scatter over the edamame beans and beansprouts. Place the peppers, spring onion and red chilli (if using) in a small bowl and mix.

When the chicken is cooked, divide it between each salad, placing it in the centre – you can serve the chicken warm or cold, whichever you prefer. Top with the pepper, spring onion and red chilli mixture, scattering it over the chicken and salad. Drizzle each salad with 2 tablespoons of sweet chilli sauce and serve at once, with lime slices on the side if you like.

TIPS:
Toasting the sea salt gives the chicken nuggets an authentic salt and pepper flavour.
You can use 150g of frozen edamame beans, cooked according to packet instructions, and cooled.

QUICK PREP

MUSHROOM KEEMA

🕐 **10 MINS**　　🍲 **35 MINS**　　✕ **SERVES 4**

PER SERVING:
180 KCAL / 28G CARBS

600g chestnut mushrooms
low-calorie cooking spray
1 large onion, peeled and finely chopped
4 garlic cloves, peeled and crushed
3cm (1¼in) piece of root ginger, peeled and grated
1 tbsp medium curry powder
250g potatoes, peeled and cut into 1cm (½in) dice
1 x 400g tin chopped tomatoes
1 tbsp Henderson's relish
1 vegetable stock cube
150g frozen peas
sea salt and freshly ground black pepper
handful of fresh coriander leaves, chopped
1 tbsp mango chutney

TO ACCOMPANY
50g uncooked basmati rice per portion, cooked according to packet instructions (+ 173 kcal per 125g cooked serving)

Inspired by one of our favourite takeaway orders, this easy recipe is a vegetarian twist on a keema-style curry. Instead of minced meat, we've used budget-friendly, low-calorie mushrooms. You won't want to miss out the splash of Henderson's relish – you might think it's an unusual ingredient for a curry, but trust us, it really brings out the umami flavours of the mushrooms.

Everyday Light

Finely chop the mushrooms. You want a texture that looks like Quorn mince. The pulse setting on a food processor is ideal for this, and will save time, but you can use a knife if you wish.

Spray a large saucepan (which has a tight-fitting lid) with low-calorie cooking spray and place over a medium heat. Add the onion and fry for about 8 minutes, until soft and beginning to colour, then add the garlic and ginger and cook for a further 2 minutes. Add the curry powder, mushrooms, potatoes, chopped tomatoes and Henderson's relish, and crumble the stock cube straight into the pan (there's no need to dissolve it in water). Increase the heat and bring to the boil while stirring. It may look a bit dry at this stage, but the mushrooms will release liquid as they cook to produce a rich sauce.

When the pan is bubbling rapidly, cover with a tight-fitting lid and reduce the heat to medium. Cook for 20 minutes, stirring halfway through.

After 20 minutes, stir in the frozen peas, bring back to a rapid simmer and continue to cook, uncovered, for a further 5 minutes, or until the potatoes are soft and the sauce is thick and rich.

Stir in the mango chutney and coriander, taste and season with salt and pepper if required, then serve with rice.

VEGGIE

VEGAN

USE RAMEN NOODLES

FREEZE ME

BROTH ONLY

BATCH COOK

DAIRY FREE

GLUTEN FREE

USE GF STOCK CUBE

BACON AND RED PESTO SOUP

🕐 **10 MINS**　　🍲 **40 MINS**　　✕ **SERVES 4**

PER SERVING:
292 KCAL / 30G CARBS

low-calorie cooking spray
2 medium onions, peeled and
　chopped
2 garlic cloves, peeled and
　crushed
4 smoked bacon medallions, cut
　into 1cm (½in) dice
1 litre chicken stock (2 chicken
　stock cubes dissolved in 1 litre
　boiling water)
500g potatoes, peeled and cut
　into 1cm (½in) dice
5 tbsp red pesto sauce
5g fresh basil leaves, stalks
　removed and leaves roughly
　chopped
sea salt and freshly ground
　black pepper

TO SERVE (OPTIONAL)
4 tsp red pesto
handful of roughly torn basil
　leaves

TO ACCOMPANY (OPTIONAL)
60g wholemeal bread rolls
　(+ 146 kcal per roll)

You can make this thick and tasty soup with just a few simple ingredients. We've used readymade red pesto sauce from a jar to add a boost of red pepper and tomato flavours to the soup. Top your steaming bowl of soup with a little extra red pesto and swirl it in if you would like to make it more indulgent, but don't forget to adjust the calories (see tip)!

Everyday Light ─────────────────

Spray a large saucepan with low-calorie cooking spray and place over a medium heat. Add the onion and cook for 5 minutes until it starts to soften, then add the garlic and cook for a further 1–2 minutes.

Add the bacon and cook for 3–4 minutes until the bacon is cooked and the onions are soft. Add the stock, potatoes and red pesto and stir. Cover with a lid and bring to the boil then reduce the heat and simmer, covered, for 25–30 minutes until the potatoes are soft.

Remove from the heat and blitz in a food processor or with a stick blender until smooth. Depending on the size of your food processor, you may need to do this in several batches. Stir in the basil and season to taste, if needed. Transfer to serving bowls and swirl a teaspoonful of red pesto sauce on top of each and sprinkle with fresh basil leaves, if you like.

The soup will keep in the fridge for 1–2 days. To freeze, follow standard guidelines for defrosting and reheating.

TIP:

Just before serving, you can add a teaspoonful of red pesto sauce to your bowl of soup and swirl it on top. This would add another 26 kcal per serving.

QUICK PREP

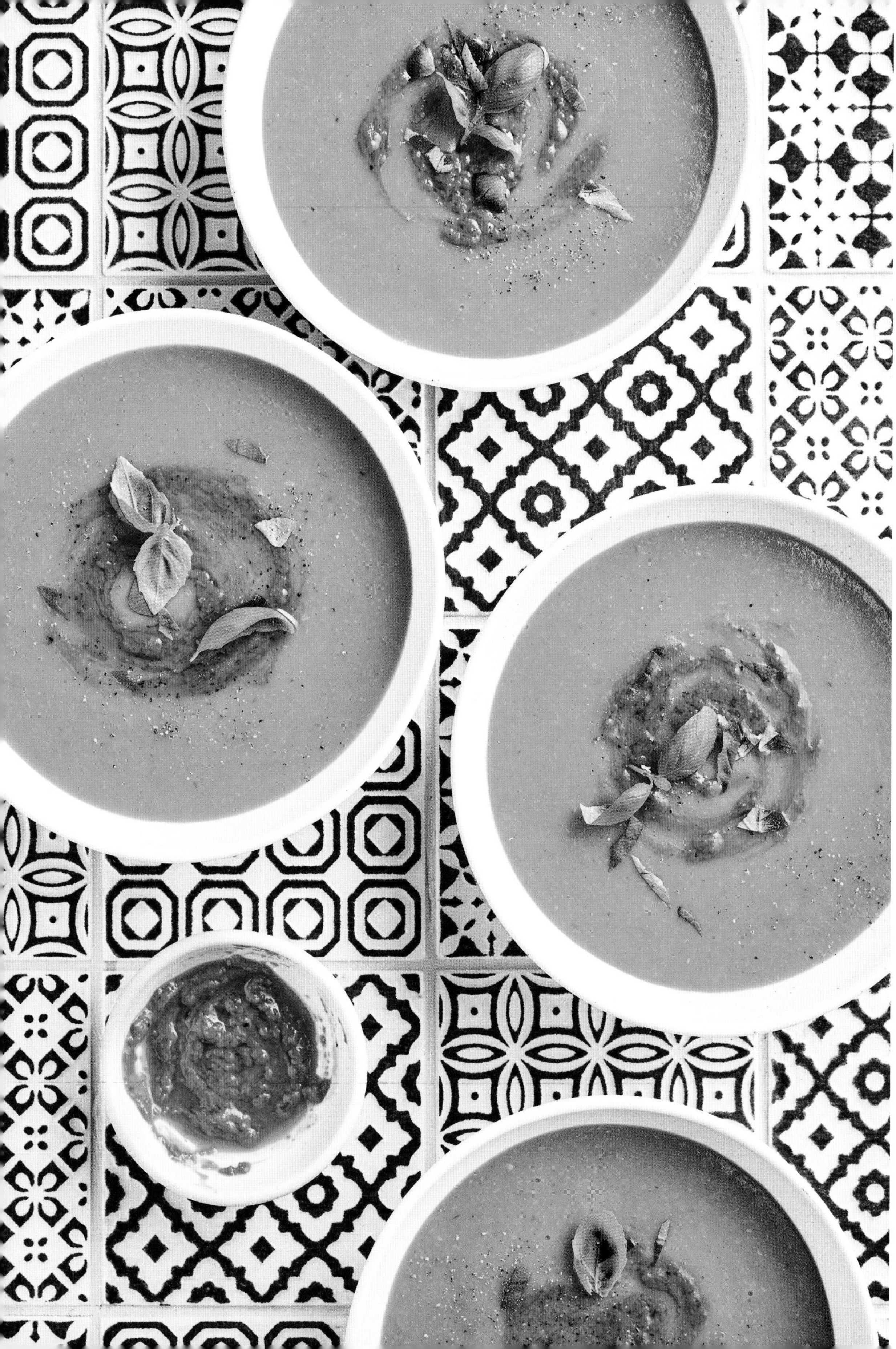

CULLEN SKINK

🕐 **10 MINS**　🍲 **30 MINS**　✕ **SERVES 4**

PER SERVING:
246 KCAL /33G CARBS

low-calorie cooking spray
½ medium onion, peeled and
　finely diced
2 leeks, trimmed and thinly
　sliced
300g skinless, boneless smoked
　haddock (undyed haddock is
　preferable)
2 dried bay leaves
500ml skimmed milk
550g potatoes, peeled and cut
　into 1cm (½in) dice
500ml fish or vegetable stock
　(1 fish or vegetable stock cube
　dissolved in 500ml boiling
　water)
2 tsp lemon juice
10g fresh chives, snipped
sea salt and freshly ground
　black pepper

TO ACCOMPANY (OPTIONAL)
60g wholemeal bread rolls
　(+ 146 kcal per roll)

Cullen Skink is a comforting Scottish recipe, similar to a chowder. To keep things slimming friendly, we've simmered onion, leeks and potatoes in skimmed milk until our smoked haddock fillets are delightfully flaky. This hearty soup is best when it has a bit of texture, so don't be afraid to leave your potatoes lightly mashed with chunks in! You'll want to ladle this one into bowls with chopped chives sprinkled on top.

Everyday Light ————————————————————

Spray a large saucepan with low-calorie cooking spray and place over a low heat. Add the onion and leeks and sauté gently for 15 minutes, stirring occasionally.

While the onion and leeks cook, place the smoked haddock and bay leaves in a shallow pan and cover with the milk. Bring to a gentle simmer, taking care not to let it boil, and cook for 5 minutes until the fish is just cooked. Remove the fish from the pan and cover. Don't discard the milk as you will need it in the next step.

When the onion and leeks are softened, add the potatoes, stock and milk, including the bay leaves. Simmer gently for 15 minutes, until the potatoes are soft.

Remove the bay leaves. You can blend the soup with a stick blender now, if you wish, but we prefer a more textured soup, so use a potato masher to lightly mash the potatoes, keeping a few chunks intact. Flake the cooked haddock into the soup, and stir in the lemon juice and chives, reserving a few for garnish.

Taste the soup and season with salt and pepper if needed. Ladle into bowls, sprinkle on the reserved chives and serve with wholemeal bread rolls, if you wish.

The soup will keep in the fridge for up to 3 days, and can also be frozen. To freeze, follow standard guidelines for defrosting and reheating.

QUICK PREP

VEGGIE

VEGAN

USE VEGAN
STOCK CUBE

FREEZE
ME

BATCH
COOK

DAIRY
FREE

GLUTEN
FREE

USE GF STOCK
CUBE

ROASTED ROOT VEGETABLE SOUP

🕐 **15 MINS**   🍲 **1 HOUR 5 MINS**   ✕ **SERVES 4**

PER SERVING:
120 KCAL / 19G CARBS

250g carrots, peeled and
   roughly chopped
250g swede, peeled and
   roughly chopped
150g potato, peeled and
   roughly chopped
1 onion, peeled and roughly
   chopped
1 leek, trimmed and cut into
   chunky slices
6 garlic cloves (no need to peel)
low-calorie cooking spray
handful of fresh thyme sprigs,
   stalks removed
1.2 litres vegetable stock
   (2 vegetable stock cubes
   dissolved in 1.2 litres boiling
   water)
juice of ½ lemon
sea salt and freshly ground
   black pepper

TO ACCOMPANY (OPTIONAL)
50g piece of fresh baguette
   (+ 137 kcal per piece)

A warming bowl of soup is just what you need on a chilly day. This one is especially filling, despite being so low in calories. Roasting your vegetables in the oven before adding them to the stock is a great way to bring out bigger, more intense flavours. The roasted garlic and herby thyme come through in every spoonful, taking this simple soup up a notch. Ideal for batch cooking, you'll always be pleased to find a portion of this in your freezer!

Everyday Light

Preheat the oven to 220°C (fan 200°C/gas mark 7).

Place all the vegetables, including the whole garlic cloves, in a large bowl and spray well with low-calorie cooking spray. Season with salt and pepper and toss around to well coat the vegetables. Scatter over a baking tray and roast in the oven for 35 minutes, shaking halfway through to ensure even browning.

Remove the vegetables from the oven. They should be lightly coloured. Don't worry if they are not soft, as we will be cooking them further on the hob.

Remove the garlic from the tray and remove the skin. Place the peeled garlic in a large saucepan and add the roasted vegetables, most of the thyme leaves and all the stock. Bring to the boil, then reduce the heat to a simmer, cover and cook for 30 minutes.

Remove from the heat and add the lemon juice, then blitz the soup until smooth, in a food processor or with a hand blender, being careful not to splash yourself.

This soup should be thick, but if it is too thick for your liking, add a little boiling water. Bear in mind that the more water you add, the less intense the flavours will be.

Ladle into bowls and garnish with the remaining thyme leaves. Serve with a piece of fresh baguette or other accompaniment of your choice.

The soup will keep in the fridge for up to up to 3 days. To freeze, follow standard guidelines for defrosting and reheating.

QUICK PREP

152

SPICY PASTA SOUP

🕐 **15 MINS**　🍲 **45 MINS**　✕ **SERVES 4**

VEGGIE

VEGAN

USE VEGAN STOCK CUBES/ POT

FREEZE ME

BATCH COOK

DAIRY FREE

GLUTEN FREE

USE GF PASTA AND STOCK CUBES/POT

PER SERVING:
274 KCAL / 44G CARBS

low-calorie cooking spray
1 medium onion, peeled and diced
2 carrots, peeled and cut into 1cm (½in) dice
1 pepper, deseeded and diced
1 courgette, cut into 1cm (½in) dice
2 garlic cloves, peeled and crushed
1 or 2 chillies (depending on how spicy you like it), seeds left in and finely diced
2 tsp dried Italian herbs
1 tsp smoked paprika
2 tbsp tomato puree
1 x 400g tin chopped tomatoes
1 tbsp balsamic vinegar
1.2 litres vegetable stock (2 vegetable stock cubes dissolved in 1.2 litres boiling water)
1 red wine stock pot (optional)
1 x 400g tin mixed beans in water, drained and rinsed
100g small, dried pasta shapes, e.g. macaroni

TO ACCOMPANY (OPTIONAL)
60g wholemeal bread rolls (+ 146 kcal per roll)

When you can't decide what to have for lunch, let this budget-friendly soup make your mind up for you! A tasty way to clear out your store cupboard, it'll transform your unloved tinned beans and dried pasta shapes into a filling, flavoursome one-pot. It'll be love at first slurp, with or without a crusty bread roll involved. It's so good, we're always making extra to stock up the freezer!

Everyday Light ───────────────

Spray a large saucepan with low-calorie cooking spray and place over a medium heat. Add the onion, carrots, pepper and courgette and sauté for 8 minutes, until beginning to soften, then add the garlic, diced chilli, Italian herbs and paprika and cook for a further 2 minutes. Stir in the tomato puree, chopped tomatoes, balsamic vinegar and stock and red wine stock pot (if using). Bring to the boil then reduce the heat to a simmer and cook for 20 minutes, until the carrots are soft.

After 20 minutes, add the beans and the pasta and continue to cook for a further 10–12 minutes until the pasta is cooked through. Serve with a wholemeal bread roll if you wish.

The soup will keep in the fridge for up to 3 days. To freeze, follow standard guidelines for defrosting and reheating. The pasta can absorb some of the liquid as it reheats so you may find the soup a bit dry. Add some extra stock as you reheat.

CREAMY BACON AND BUTTERNUT SQUASH CHICKEN

🕐 **10 MINS**   🍲 **25 MINS**   ✕ **SERVES 4**

PER SERVING:
278 KCAL /15G CARBS

400g butternut squash, peeled and cut into 2cm (¾in) cubes
low-calorie cooking spray
1 medium onion, peeled and finely chopped
2 garlic cloves, peeled and crushed
400g diced chicken breast
4 smoked bacon medallions, cut into 2cm (¾in) dice
400ml chicken stock (1 very low-salt chicken stock cube dissolved in 400ml boiling water)
2 tsp dried sage
2 tbsp Dijon mustard
¼ tsp English mustard powder
175g reduced-fat cream cheese
40g baby spinach leaves
freshly ground black pepper

TO ACCOMPANY
Creamy Mashed Potatoes from the Pinch of Nom website (+ 176 kcal per serving)

With smoky bacon and sweet butternut squash, this chicken recipe is perfect for a quick midweek meal. The creamy sauce is a tasty combination of chicken stock, Dijon mustard, sage and reduced-fat cream cheese. At 278 calories per serving, we like to serve it with a side of mashed potatoes, but it's delicious with pasta too!

Weekly Indulgence

Put the butternut squash in a medium saucepan and cover with cold water. Place over a high heat, cover and bring to the boil, then reduce the heat and simmer for 8–10 minutes, or until just tender. Drain well and set aside.

While the butternut squash is cooking, spray a large frying pan with low-calorie cooking spray and place over a medium heat. Add the onion and garlic and fry for about 5 minutes until softened a little, then add the chicken and bacon and cook for 4–5 minutes until lightly browned all over. Add the stock, sage, Dijon mustard, mustard powder and cooked butternut squash. Stir, then simmer gently, uncovered, over a medium heat for 15 minutes until the chicken is cooked, shows no sign of pinkness and the juices run clear.

Remove from the heat and stir in the cream cheese until completely blended in. If the sauce is too thin for your taste, continue simmering, uncovered, for a few minutes longer until reduced and thickened a little. If the sauce is too thick for your taste, stir in a little water to thin it.

Return to the heat and stir in the baby spinach leaves, for a minute or two, until just wilted. Taste and season with freshly ground black pepper, if needed. (We found no salt was needed as the bacon provides saltiness in this dish.) Serve with a portion of Creamy Mashed Potatoes or a small portion of pasta.

TIP:

We recommend a reduced-fat cream cheese rather than a low-fat one. The result is richer and stands up better to reheating if you plan to batch cook this recipe.

QUICK PREP

TOMATO AND MANGO SALSA CHICKEN

🕐 **10 MINS**　　🍲 **30 MINS**　　✕ **SERVES 4**

PER SERVING:
232 KCAL /12G CARBS

SPECIAL EQUIPMENT
Large ovenproof dish
(about 18 x 27cm/7 x 10½in)

low-calorie cooking spray
4 skinless, boneless chicken
　breasts (about 130g each)
40g reduced-fat mature
　Cheddar, finely grated
sea salt and freshly ground
　black pepper
5g fresh coriander leaves,
　roughly chopped, to serve

FOR THE SALSA
½ red onion, peeled and cut into
　chunks
½ red chilli, deseeded
2 tomatoes, cut into chunks
90g roasted red pepper (in
　brine, from a jar), drained and
　cut into chunks
150g fresh ripe mango, stoned,
　peeled and cut into chunks
2 garlic cloves, peeled and
　crushed
1 tbsp tomato puree
1 tsp lime juice, plus slices for
　garnish (optional)
¼ tsp white granulated
　sweetener

TO ACCOMPANY
50g uncooked basmati rice per
　portion, cooked according to
　packet instructions (+ 173 kcal
　per 125g cooked serving)

This cheesy baked chicken has a fruity secret! Our homemade salsa of tomatoes and fresh mango is hidden underneath the golden topping, and you'll be obsessed with the sweet and tangy flavour it adds. This is a midweek dinner staple, quick to prep and easy to pair with a side salad, rice, chips or roast potatoes. Try adding a spoonful of the Roasted Lemon and Parmesan Broccoli from page 72!

Weekly Indulgence ————————————————————

Preheat the oven to 200°C (fan 180°C/gas mark 6).

To make the salsa, blitz the red onion and chilli in a food processor until coarsely chopped, or chop by hand, then scrape into a mixing bowl. Place the tomatoes, red pepper and mango in the food processor and blitz again until coarsely chopped. This won't take as long to chop as the onion and chilli, so take care not to over-process. Add to the onion and chilli in the mixing bowl. Add the garlic, tomato puree, lime juice and sweetener to the bowl. Season with salt and black pepper and stir well.

Spray a frying pan with low-calorie cooking spray and place over a medium-high heat. When the frying pan is hot, add the chicken breasts and seal for about 2 minutes on each side, until golden, then arrange them in the ovenproof dish. Spoon the tomato and mango salsa over the chicken breasts and sprinkle over the grated cheese. Bake in the oven for 25–30 minutes, or until the chicken is cooked through, shows no sign of pinkness, and the cheese is melted and golden.

Scatter over the chopped coriander, garnish with lime slices if you like and serve with rice.

The dish will keep in fridge for up to 3 days. To freeze, cool as quickly as possible then divide into individual portions. Freeze in individual freezerproof containers. Defrost in the fridge overnight and reheat in the microwave until piping hot throughout.

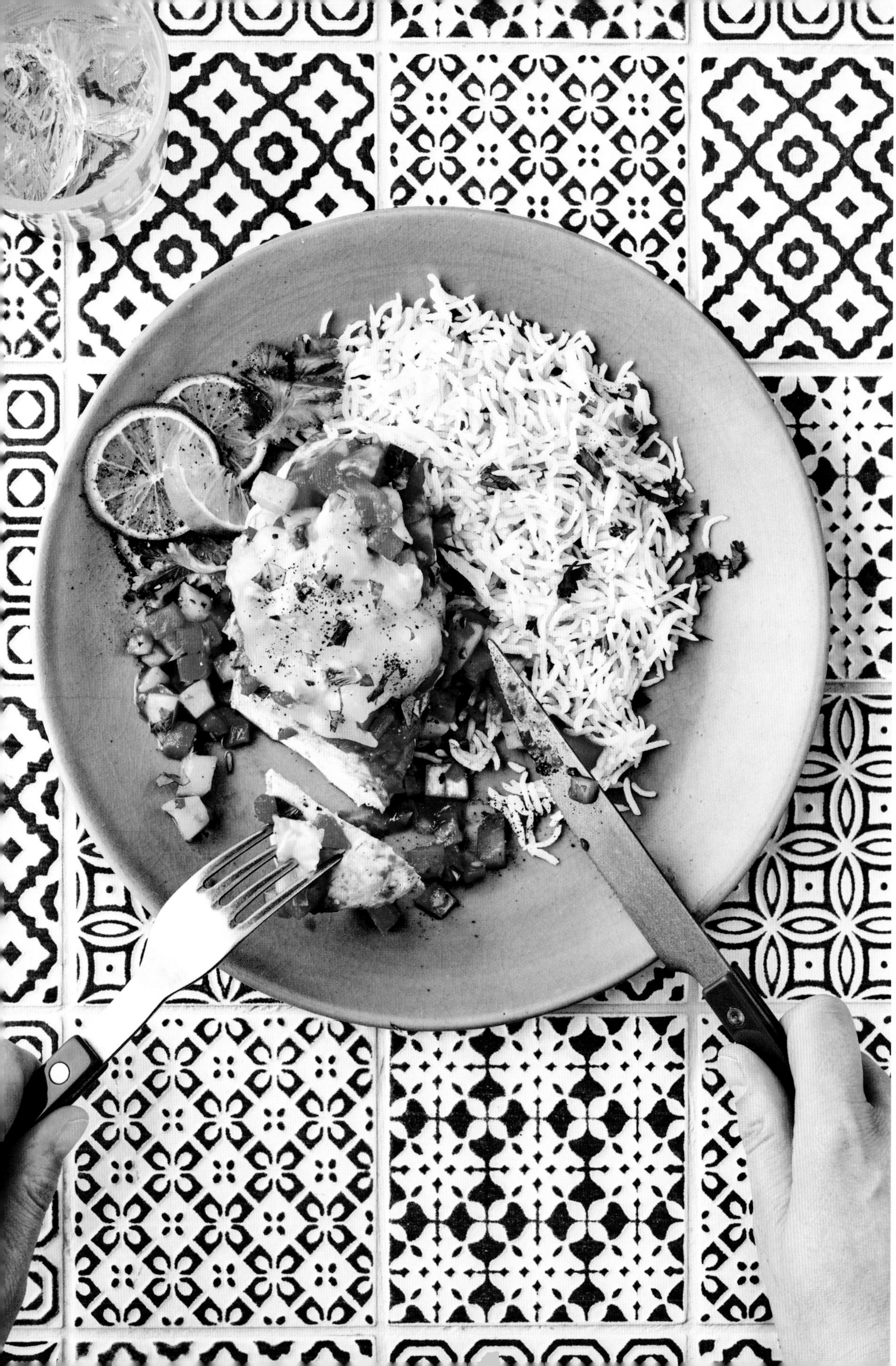

CHEESY MARMITE PASTA BAKE

⏱ **10 MINS**　🍲 **30 MINS**　✕ **SERVES 4**

PER SERVING:
499 KCAL /57G CARBS

SPECIAL EQUIPMENT
Ovenproof dish, about 28 x 24cm (11 x 9½in)

6 reduced-fat pork sausages (about 400g)
250g dried pasta shapes
2–3 tsp Marmite or other yeast extract
200ml boiling water
1 tbsp cornflour
180g reduced-fat spreadable cheese
80g reduced-fat mature Cheddar, finely grated
pinch of freshly ground black pepper

TO ACCOMPANY
75g mixed salad (+ 15 kcal per serving)

Homemade sausage meatballs and a sneaky dollop of Marmite really take this speedy pasta bake to the next level. Love it or hate it, the deep, savoury flavour of Marmite works so well in this recipe, melting into the creamy, cheesy sauce. Ideal for a busy midweek day, it's on the table in just over half an hour, and it's guaranteed to be a crowd-pleaser. Serve with a simple side salad for a really hearty, easy dinner.

Special Occasion ———————————————

Preheat the oven to 200°C (fan 180°C/gas mark 6).

Squeeze the sausage meat out of the skins and roll into 24 evenly sized balls. Place on a baking tray and bake in the oven for 12–15 minutes, until cooked through.

Meanwhile, cook the pasta according to the packet instructions. This will usually take 9–12 minutes in boiling water. Drain and set to one side while you prepare the sauce.

Dissolve the Marmite in 200ml of boiling water. Mix the cornflour with 1 tablespoon of cold water in a separate bowl.

Return the empty pasta pan to the heat, add the spreadable cheese and Marmite stock and whisk well, until all the cheese has melted. Whisk in the cornflour slurry to thicken the sauce and allow to bubble for a minute or two.

Stir in half the grated cheese until melted, then stir in the pasta and the sausage meatballs, season with the pinch of black pepper, then pour into the ovenproof dish. Sprinkle over the remaining grated cheese and bake in the oven for 15 minutes, until the top is melted and golden. Serve with a mixed salad.

The bake will keep in the fridge for up to 3 days. To freeze, follow standard guidelines for defrosting and reheating.

QUICK PREP

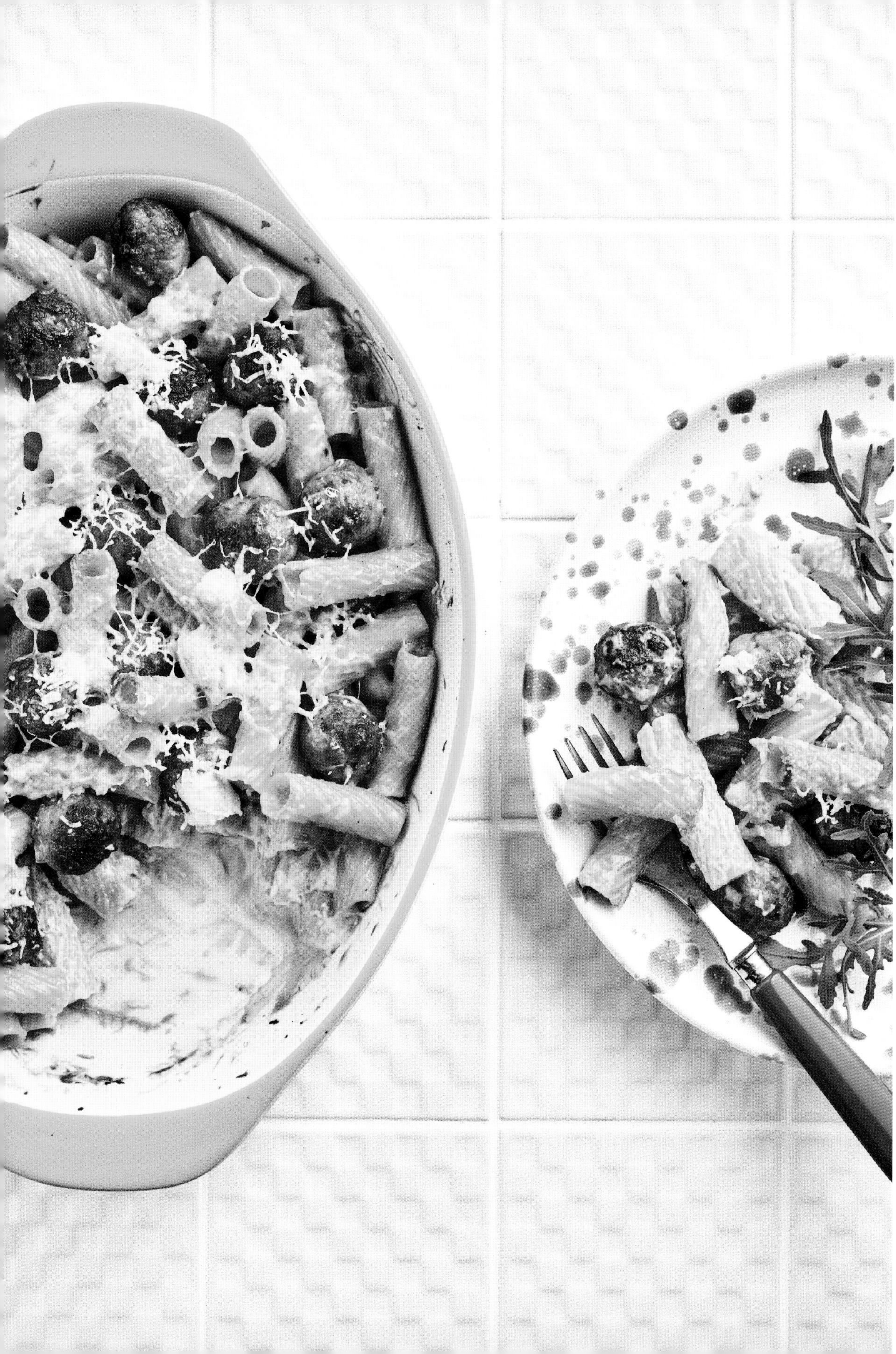

HAM AND LEEK GRATIN

🕐 **15 MINS**   🍲 **45 MINS**   ✕ **SERVES 4**

PER SERVING:
373 KCAL / 28G CARBS

SPECIAL EQUIPMENT
Ovenproof dish, about
28 x 20cm (11 x 8in)

FOR THE FILLING
low-calorie cooking spray
4 large leeks, trimmed and
    thinly sliced
200g sliced cooked smoked
    ham, diced
80g frozen peas
1 tsp garlic granules
1 tsp mustard powder

FOR THE CHEESE SAUCE
500ml semi-skimmed milk
25g reduced-fat spread
3 tbsp cornflour
100g reduced-fat mature
    Cheddar, finely grated
¼ tsp mustard powder

FOR THE TOPPING
1 medium slice of wholemeal
    bread
20g reduced-fat Cheddar,
    finely grated
1 tsp garlic granules
sea salt and freshly ground
    black pepper
2 tbsp chopped curly parsley
    leaves (optional)

TO ACCOMPANY
80g steamed vegetables
(+ 38 kcal per serving)

This hearty bake has everything you want from a plate of comfort food. From the creamy, cheesy sauce to the crispy golden topping, it doesn't feel (or taste) like slimming-friendly food. Ham and leeks are mixed into our velvety homemade sauce, which uses semi-skimmed milk and reduced-fat cheese to keep the calories down.

Weekly Indulgence ———————————————

Preheat the oven to 200°C (fan 180°C/gas mark 6). Spray a large, deep frying pan with low-calorie cooking spray and place over a low-medium heat. Add the leeks and fry gently for 20 minutes, until soft and golden.

Stir in the ham, frozen peas, garlic granules and mustard powder, season to taste with salt and pepper, then place the filling in the ovenproof dish and spread it out evenly.

While the filling is cooking, make the cheese sauce. Pour the milk into a small saucepan, add the reduced-fat spread and heat gently until steaming hot and the reduced-fat spread has melted. Take care not to let the milk boil over.

Place the cornflour in a small bowl, add 3 tablespoons of cold water and mix until smooth. Pour the cornflour mixture into the hot milk, stirring constantly with a balloon whisk. Bring to the boil then immediately reduce the heat and simmer for 3–5 minutes, stirring, until the sauce is smooth and thickened. Stir in the grated cheese and mustard powder until the cheese has melted and the sauce is smooth. Season to taste with salt and pepper. Pour the cheese sauce evenly over the ham and leek filling in the ovenproof dish and stir to completely combine.

Blitz the bread in a food processor, or use a stick blender, until it resembles fine breadcrumbs. Place the breadcrumbs in a small bowl and add the grated cheese, garlic granules and season to taste with salt and pepper. Mix well then sprinkle over the filling in the ovenproof dish.

Place in the preheated oven for 25 minutes until lightly browned and the filling is bubbling. Sprinkle with chopped parsley, to garnish (if using), and serve with steamed green vegetables.

SPANISH-STYLE ROAST VEGETABLES

🕐 **15 MINS**   🍲 **30 MINS**   ✕ **SERVES 2**

PER SERVING:
137 KCAL /19G CARBS

1 aubergine, stalk removed and
   cut in half lengthways
2 courgettes, stalks removed
   and cut into chunky batons
200g cherry tomatoes
1 red onion, peeled and
   quartered
1 pepper (any colour), deseeded
   and cut into 5cm (2in) pieces
4 garlic cloves, peeled and
   crushed
low-calorie cooking spray
¼ tsp onion granules
a few sprigs of thyme, leaves
   removed from stalk
sea salt and freshly ground
   black pepper
5g fresh basil leaves, roughly
   torn, to granish

Inspired by the popular Spanish dish escalivada, this easy
vegan recipe is a simple medley of roasted vegetables,
finished under the grill for a lovely char. Well seasoned and
sprinkled with thyme and basil, this recipe doesn't scrimp
on flavour. It's so versatile that you can enjoy it as a light
lunch, dinner or side dish – it's up to you!

Everyday Light ─────────────────────

Preheat the oven to 220°C (fan 200°C/gas mark 7).

Take one half of the aubergine and cut it into 4 lengths.
Repeat with the other half and lay onto a large baking
tray. Add the courgettes, cherry tomatoes, onion quarters,
pepper and garlic. Spray with low-calorie cooking spray,
sprinkle with the onion granules, season with salt and
pepper and toss to coat. Bake in the oven for 15 minutes.

After 15 minutes, remove from the oven and turn on the
grill. Add most of the thyme leaves and pop under the grill
for about 15 minutes, or until the pepper skin is starting to
blacken and the vegetables are soft and beginning to char
around the edges.

Scatter over the torn basil and remaining thyme leaves
and serve.

VEGGIE

VEGAN

USE PLANT-
BASED MINCE
AND A VEGAN
BEEF-FLAVOUR
STOCK CUBE

FREEZE
ME

BATCH
COOK

DAIRY
FREE

GLUTEN
FREE

USE GF STOCK
CUBE

BBQ BOLOGNESE

⏰ **10 MINS**　　🍲 **45 MINS**　　✕ **SERVES 4**

PER SERVING:
284 KCAL / 19G CARBS

low-calorie cooking spray
1 medium onion, peeled
　and diced
3 garlic cloves, peeled
　and crushed
1 medium carrot, peeled
　and diced
1 red pepper, deseeded
　and diced
500g 5%-fat minced beef
200ml beef stock (1 beef
　stock cube dissolved in
　200ml boiling water)
2 tbsp tomato puree
2 tbsp Henderson's relish
1 x 400g tin chopped tomatoes
1 tsp white granulated
　sweetener
2 tbsp BBQ seasoning
2 tbsp smoked paprika
sea salt and freshly ground
　black pepper

TO ACCOMPANY
small portion of pasta (50g dry
　weight / 100g cooked weight)
　(+ 174 kcal per serving)

We never get bored of finding fresh ways to make spag bol even better! BBQ seasoning and sweet smoked paprika makes a gorgeous, smoky-flavoured sauce that'll transform one pack of mince into a batch-cookable family favourite. Enjoy it with the fun of twisting spaghetti around your fork or serve it with any pasta shape – you won't regret wiping your plate clean with some crusty garlic bread . . .

Weekly Indulgence ────────────

Spray a large frying pan with low-calorie cooking spray and place over a medium heat. Add the onion, garlic and carrot and cook for 5 minutes until the onion is starting to soften, then add the red pepper and fry for another 4 minutes. Add the beef and cook for about 5 minutes or until browned on all sides, breaking up the mince with a wooden spoon.

Add the stock, tomato puree, Henderson's relish, chopped tomatoes, sweetener, BBQ seasoning and smoked paprika and stir well. Reduce the heat and simmer for 30 minutes until the mixture has thickened and the vegetables are soft. Season to taste with salt and pepper.

Serve with pasta.

QUICK PREP

USE DAIRY-FREE
ITALIAN HARD
CHEESE

USE GF STOCK
POT

CHICKEN PUTTANESCA BAKE

🕐 **10 MINS**   🗑 **30 MINS**   ✕ **SERVES 4**

PER SERVING:
265 KCAL / 13G CARBS

SPECIAL EQUIPMENT
Shallow casserole dish,
suitable for oven and hob,
about 26cm (10in)

low-calorie cooking spray
4 skinless, boneless chicken
  breasts (about 150g each)
1 medium onion, peeled and
  thinly sliced
2 garlic cloves, peeled and
  crushed
1 x 400g tin chopped tomatoes
20 pitted black olives, sliced
1 tbsp capers, drained
pinch of dried chilli flakes
1 red wine stock pot (or
  1 chicken stock pot plus 2 tsp
  red wine vinegar)
small handful of fresh basil
  leaves, roughly chopped, plus a
  few whole leaves to serve
1 red pepper, deseeded and
  thinly sliced
10 cherry tomatoes, halved
15g Parmesan, finely grated

TO ACCOMPANY
small portion of pasta (50g dry
  weight / 100g cooked weight)
  (+ 174 kcal per serving)

Puttanesca is an Italian-style tomato-based sauce, made with salty olives and capers to give it a distinctive, punchy umami taste. Often served with spaghetti, we think it's too delicious to save for pasta night, so we've spooned it over chicken and baked it to soak up all the rich flavours. Whether you plate it up with vegetables, crispy potatoes, salad, or your favourite pasta, you're in for a treat!

Weekly Indulgence ————————————————

Preheat the oven to 200°C (fan 180°C/gas mark 6).

Spray the shallow ovenproof casserole dish with low-calorie cooking spray and place over a medium-high heat. Add the chicken breasts and cook for 2 minutes on each side, until sealed and lightly browned, then remove from the pan and set aside.

Reduce the heat to medium-low, add the onion and sauté for 5 minutes until it begins to soften, then add the garlic and cook for another minute. Add the chopped tomatoes, olives, capers and chilli flakes, then stir in the stock pot until it dissolves (there's no need to make this up with water first). Stir in the chopped basil, then place the chicken breasts back in the pan. Scatter over the sliced pepper and halved cherry tomatoes, sprinkle over the Parmesan, then bake in the oven for 20 minutes, until the chicken is cooked through, no pinkness remains, and the juices run clear.

Remove from the oven and garnish with the reserved basil leaves. Serve with pasta.

VEGGIE
USE VEGGIE SAUSAGES

FREEZE ME

BATCH COOK

DAIRY FREE
USE DF CREAM CHEESE

GLUTEN FREE
USE GF STOCK CUBE AND SAUSAGES

CREAMY SAUSAGE AND MASH PIE

🕐 **10 MINS**　　🍲 **40 MINS**　　✕ **SERVES 4**

PER SERVING:
400 KCAL /50G CARBS

SPECIAL EQUIPMENT
Large ovenproof dish,
about 30 x 20cm (12 x 8in)

low-calorie cooking spray
6 reduced-fat pork sausages
　(about 400g), sliced into 5
　pieces
1 leek, trimmed and thinly sliced
1 carrot, peeled and diced
1 garlic clove, peeled and crushed
100g mushrooms, sliced
1 eating apple, cored and diced
　(no need to peel)
200ml vegetable stock (1
　vegetable stock cube dissolved
　in 200ml boiling water)
½ tsp mustard powder
1 tsp dried sage
100g frozen peas
150g reduced-fat cream cheese
sea salt and freshly ground
　black pepper

FOR THE MASH
650g potatoes, peeled and cut
　into chunks
½ tsp mustard powder
15g reduced-fat cream cheese

TO ACCOMPANY (OPTIONAL)
80g steamed vegetables
　(+ 38 kcal per serving)

> **TIP:**
> You could sprinkle
> 60g of finely grated
> reduced-fat Cheddar on
> top! Each portion will
> increase to 447 kcal.

When you're in the mood for a hearty, low-fuss dinner, our Creamy Sausage and Mash Pie is just the ticket. To make our filling satisfying and slimming friendly, we've combined reduced-fat sausages with leek, carrot, mushrooms and diced apple. Once it's topped with a golden layer of mustardy, cream cheese mashed potatoes, sit back and relax while your oven works its magic.

Weekly Indulgence ————————————

Preheat the oven to 210°C (fan 190°C/gas mark 6).

Add the potatoes to a saucepan and cover with cold, salted water. Bring to the boil and cook for 15–20 minutes or until the potatoes are tender. Drain well.

While the potatoes are cooking, spray a large frying pan with low-calorie cooking spray and place over a medium heat. Add the sausages, leek, carrot and garlic and cook for 5 minutes until the sausages have started to brown and the leeks and carrot start to soften. Add the mushrooms and apple and fry for a further 4 minutes. Add the stock, mustard powder and sage to the pan and stir. Reduce the heat and simmer for 10 minutes until the vegetables are soft. Remove from the heat and add the frozen peas and cream cheese. Stir until blended then season with salt and pepper. Set aside while you prepare the mash.

Mash the potatoes. Add the mustard powder and cream cheese to the mash and mix through. Season with salt and pepper, to taste.

Add the sausage mixture to the ovenproof dish and spread it out. Spoon the mash onto the top and use a fork to rough up the surface. Bake in the oven for 20 minutes until the potato is just turning golden brown, then serve with your choice of accompaniment.

The dish will keep in fridge for up to 2 days. To freeze, follow standard guidelines for defrosting and reheating.

QUICK PREP

APPLE AND MUSTARD SWINEHERD'S PIE

🕐 **15 MINS**   🍲 **45 MINS**   ✕ **SERVES 4**

PER SERVING:
431 KCAL /53G CARBS

SPECIAL EQUIPMENT
Large ovenproof dish (about 18 x 27cm/7 x 10½in) or 4 individual ovenproof dishes (about 10 x 14cm/4 x 5½in)

FOR THE FILLING
low-calorie cooking spray
2 onions, peeled and diced
2 carrots, peeled and finely diced
500g 5%-fat minced pork
1 tbsp Henderson's relish or Worcestershire sauce
1 tsp dried sage
½ tsp mustard powder
200ml pork or ham stock (2 pork or ham stock cubes dissolved in 200ml boiling water)
2 tbsp tomato puree
150g frozen peas
sea salt and freshly ground black pepper

FOR THE MASH
800g potatoes, peeled and quartered
2 tbsp readymade apple sauce
½ tsp mustard powder

TO ACCOMPANY (OPTIONAL)
80g steamed vegetables (+ 38 kcal per serving)

TIP:
If you don't have pork or ham stock, you can use chicken or beef instead.

Our twist on a British classic, this dish will warm you right up! While traditional versions might come finished with buttery mash, we've complemented our low-fat pork filling by adding apple sauce and mustard powder to our fluffy potato topping.

Weekly Indulgence

Place the potatoes for the mash in a large saucepan and cover with cold salted water. Place over a medium heat and bring to the boil then reduce the heat and boil gently for 15 minutes, or until the potatoes are cooked through and tender. Remove from the heat, drain and place a lid on the saucepan. Set aside.

Preheat the oven to 220°C (fan 200°C/gas mark 7).

While the potatoes are cooking, spray a large frying pan with low-calorie cooking spray and place over a medium heat. Add the onions and carrots and cook gently for 10 minutes, until they are beginning to soften. If the onions start to brown, reduce the heat a little. Add the mince, Henderson's relish, dried sage and mustard powder to the frying pan and cook for 5 minutes until the mince is browned, breaking up any chunks with a wooden spoon.

Add the pork or ham stock, stir well and simmer gently for 15 minutes, until the liquid has mostly reduced, and the mixture looks glossy.

Remove the frying pan from the heat and stir in the tomato puree and frozen peas. Season with salt and pepper. Set aside while you finish preparing the mash.

Add the apple sauce and mustard powder to the cooked potatoes in the saucepan. Mash until the potatoes are smooth and season with salt and pepper.

Place the filling in the ovenproof dish or ovenproof dishes and spread out evenly. Top with the mash, spread out evenly and use a fork to texture the top. Bake in the oven for 10–15 minutes or until golden brown and piping hot throughout.

Serve with steamed veg, if you like, or your accompaniment of choice.

QUICK PREP

172

STICKY PLUM AND CHICKEN TRAYBAKE

🕐 **10 MINS**   🍲 **25 MINS**   ✕ **SERVES 4**

FREEZE ME

BATCH COOK

DAIRY FREE

GLUTEN FREE

PER SERVING:
331 KCAL /15G CARBS

8 skinless, boneless chicken thighs (visible fat removed)

4 plums, stones removed and quartered

1 medium red onion, peeled and cut into 6 wedges

1 tbsp balsamic vinegar

1 tbsp honey

½ red chilli, deseeded and finely diced

2 garlic cloves, peeled and crushed

TO ACCOMPANY

50g uncooked basmati rice per portion, cooked according to packet instructions (+ 173 kcal per 125g cooked serving)

You can't beat the convenience of a traybake! You only need a short list of simple, fuss-free ingredients to make this oh-so-sticky recipe. We've combined chicken thighs and sliced plums in a punchy, chilli- and honey-infused glaze, before baking them to juicy perfection. Ready to go in 35 near-effortless minutes, the hardest part is choosing whether to serve it with salad, rice or chips.

Special Occasion ——————————————

Preheat the oven to 220°C (fan 200°C/gas mark 7).

Put the chicken thighs, plum quarters and onion wedges on a baking tray.

Combine the balsamic vinegar, honey, red chilli and garlic in a small bowl. Pour the mixture over the chicken thighs and coat well.

Bake in the oven for 12 minutes. Toss the chicken, plums and onion to coat in the sauce then return to the oven for a further 12 minutes. The plums and onion should be soft and the chicken thighs thoroughly cooked through, with no signs of pink. Serve with rice.

CHIMICHURRI BAKED COD

🕐 **15 MINS**　　🍲 **25 MINS**　　✕ **SERVES 4**

***** PLUS 30 MINS MARINATING**

PER SERVING:
179 KCAL /15G CARBS

4 boneless and skinless cod
　fillets, about 120g each
300g new potatoes
low-calorie cooking spray
½ tsp garlic granules
200g cherry tomatoes
100g green beans, trimmed
sea salt and freshly ground
　black pepper

FOR THE CHIMICHURRI
10g fresh parsley
10g fresh coriander
5g fresh mint
5g fresh oregano
juice of 1 lemon
2 garlic cloves, peeled
2 tbsp red wine vinegar
½ red chilli, deseeded
½ tsp white granulated
　sweetener

If chimichurri is involved, we're there! A really simple, tangy sauce originating from Argentina, it makes our Baked Cod into a marvellous midweek meal. Our lower-calorie version swaps oil for a combination of fresh herbs, punchy spices and vinegar, and you can hardly taste the difference! We've baked the cod inside foil parcels to guarantee they'll leave the oven flaky and flavoursome, without drying out.

Everyday Light ────────────────────

Preheat the oven to 210°C (fan 190°C/gas mark 6).

To make the chimichurri, put the parsley, coriander, mint, oregano, lemon juice, garlic, red wine vinegar and red chilli in a food processor, or use a stick blender, and blitz until finely chopped. Stir in the sweetener and season to taste with a little salt and pepper.

Cut four squares of foil, each large enough to fold over and enclose a cod fillet. Place a cod fillet into the centre of each square. Add a teaspoonful of the chimichurri mixture to the top of each fillet and spread to cover the top. Seal the fish into the foil by folding over the top and sides, put the parcels on a baking tray and leave in the fridge for 30 minutes, for the flavours to develop.

Slice the new potatoes thinly (slightly thicker than a pound coin) and add to another baking tray. Spray with low-calorie cooking spray and sprinkle over the garlic granules, season with salt and pepper and toss to coat. Pop into the oven for 10 minutes.

After 10 minutes, add the tomatoes and green beans to the tray and pop back into the oven. Add the baking tray with the fish and cook for 15 minutes.

Remove both baking trays from the oven. The potatoes should be slightly golden round the edges and the fish flaky. Remove the fish from the foil and place on serving plates with the vegetables. Drizzle the remaining chimichurri herb mix over the fish and vegetables before serving.

BOBOTIE

🕐 **10 MINS**   🍲 **1 HOUR**   ✕ **SERVES 4**

PER SERVING:
313 KCAL / 21G CARBS

SPECIAL EQUIPMENT
Large ovenproof dish (about 18 x 27cm/7 x 10½in)

FOR THE FILLING
low-calorie cooking spray
2 medium onions, peeled and chopped
4 garlic cloves, peeled and crushed
2 tbsp mild curry powder
1 tsp dried basil
1 tsp dried thyme
1 tsp dried oregano
1 tsp ground turmeric
1 tsp ground cumin
1 tsp ground coriander
500g 5%-fat minced beef
1 tbsp mango chutney
2 dried bay leaves
1 tbsp Worcestershire sauce or Henderson's relish
1 medium eating apple, cored, skin left on and coarsely grated
sea salt and freshly ground black pepper

FOR THE TOPPING
2 medium eggs, beaten
250ml skimmed milk
3 dried bay leaves

TO ACCOMPANY
80g steamed mixed vegetables (+ 38 kcal per serving) or 75g mixed salad (+ 15kcal per serving)

This is our version of a recipe that's popular in South Africa and has a mild, slightly sweet curry flavour. The curried beef is topped with a thin egg custard layer, which sounds unusual but really works. This hearty, comforting dish would be ideal for a family meal.

Everyday Light ——————————————

Preheat the oven to 200°C (fan 180°C/gas mark 6).

Spray a large frying pan with low-calorie cooking spray and place over a medium heat. Add the onions and cook gently for about 10 minutes, until softened and golden, then add the garlic, curry powder, basil, thyme, oregano, turmeric, cumin and coriander. Stir and cook for 1–2 minutes.

Add the beef and cook for 4–5 minutes, to seal on all sides, breaking up the mince with a wooden spoon. Stir in the chutney, bay leaves, Worcestershire sauce and grated apple. Lower the heat and cook, uncovered, for 15 minutes, stirring occasionally. The beef mixture won't have a sauce but will just be moist.

Remove the bay leaves and transfer the mixture to the ovenproof dish. Spread it out evenly and press it down with the back of a large spoon. This will help to keep the egg custard layer sitting on the top of the layer of beef. (The dish can be frozen at this point, without the egg custard layer, and defrosted before adding the custard layer and baking. Follow standard guidelines for defrosting and reheating.)

In a measuring jug, mix together the eggs and milk, and season with salt and pepper. Beat with a fork until evenly mixed.

Pour the egg custard mixture carefully over the beef layer, taking care not to disturb the beef. Place 3 bay leaves on top and place the dish on a baking tray. Bake in the oven for 20–25 minutes, until the egg custard is golden and just set in the middle, and the filling is piping hot throughout.

Serve at once with mixed salad, steamed vegetables or other accompaniments of your choice.

QUICK PREP

VEGGIE

USE VEGGIE
SAUSAGES AND
STOCK CUBE

**FREEZE
ME**

**BATCH
COOK**

**GLUTEN
FREE**

USE GF
SAUSAGES AND
STOCK CUBE

DIJON SAUSAGES

🕐 **10 MINS**   🍲 **45 MINS**   ✕ **SERVES 4**

**PER SERVING:
288 KCAL /19G CARBS**

low-calorie cooking spray
1 medium onion, peeled and
    thinly sliced
1 garlic clove, peeled and
    crushed
8 reduced-fat pork sausages
200g button mushrooms, sliced
300ml chicken stock (1 reduced-
    salt chicken stock cube
    dissolved in 300ml boiling
    water)
3 tbsp Dijon mustard
½ tsp mustard powder
40g frozen peas
2 tbsp reduced-fat cream
    cheese
freshly ground black pepper
2 tbsp chopped chives, to serve

TO ACCOMPANY
225g potato, baked (+ 173 kcal
    per serving)

You won't believe how easy it is to put together this creamy sausage one-pot! While it might look and taste luxurious, it only requires a short list of budget-friendly ingredients. For our silky, mustard sauce, we've simmered the sausages with reduced-fat cream cheese, punchy Dijon mustard and mustard powder. Serve with fluffy baked potatoes and put the 'bang' in Bangers and Mash!

Weekly Indulgence ————————————

Spray a large frying pan with low-calorie cooking spray and place over a medium heat. Add the onion and fry for 10–15 minutes, stirring occasionally, until softened and golden, then add the garlic and sausages and cook for 5–6 minutes, or until the sausages are browned on all sides. Add the mushrooms, chicken stock, Dijon mustard and mustard powder, stir and simmer, uncovered, for 20–25 minutes, turning the sausages occasionally. Stir in the frozen peas for the last 2–3 minutes of cooking.

The sausages should be cooked through and show no sign of pinkness inside.

Remove from the heat and stir in the cream cheese until completely blended. If the sauce is too thick for your liking, stir in a little water; if it's too thin for your liking, continue to simmer, uncovered for a few more minutes. Season to taste with black pepper, sprinkle with chopped chives and serve with an accompaniment of your choice.

QUICK PREP

CURRIED QUICHE

🕐 **10 MINS**　　🍲 **35 MINS**　　✕ **SERVES 8**

PER SERVING:
186 KCAL / 8.1G CARBS

SPECIAL EQUIPMENT
24cm (9½in) flan dish

low-calorie cooking spray
½ medium onion, peeled and
　thinly sliced
½ yellow pepper, deseeded and
　finely diced
6 medium eggs
200ml light double cream
　alternative
70g quark
1 tbsp medium curry powder
½ tsp mild chilli powder
½ tsp paprika
½ tsp ground turmeric
¼ tsp salt
¼ tsp freshly ground black
　pepper
150g cooked skinless, boneless
　chicken breast, shredded
10g fresh coriander leaves,
　chopped
3 tbsp mango chutney

TO ACCOMPANY (OPTIONAL)
75g mixed salad (+ 15 kcal per
　serving)

We wanted to make a crustless quiche so flavoursome that it'd be impossible to miss the pastry crust, and we reckon we've nailed it! With caramelised onions, sweet peppers and chicken, every bite of this curry-spiced quiche is creamy and satisfying – served hot or cold! It's not curry night without mango chutney, so we've swirled in a few sweet, tangy tablespoons to liven up the flavours.

Everyday Light ————————————————

Preheat the oven to 190°C (fan 170°C/gas mark 5).

Spray a small frying pan with low-calorie cooking spray and place over a medium heat. Add the onion and yellow pepper and cook for 5 minutes, until turning lightly golden and starting to soften. Set aside.

Break the eggs into a large bowl and whisk. Add the double cream alternative and quark and whisk again, then add the curry powder, chilli powder, paprika, turmeric, salt and pepper, and whisk to combine.

Stir in the shredded chicken, onion and yellow pepper. Pour the egg mixture into the flan dish, sprinkle over the coriander and mix lightly. Using a small spoon, dot the mango chutney onto the surface of the quiche and swirl it lightly into the quiche mixture using a knife.

Place the dish onto a baking tray and bake in the oven for 25–30 minutes, until the quiche is golden brown. The quiche should be set around the edge with a very slight wobble in the centre. The heat from the quiche will finish cooking the centre as it cools, so that it has a light, creamy texture when slicing. Serve with a mixed salad.

The quiche will keep in the fridge for up to 3 days. To freeze, cool as quickly as possible then cut into individual portions. Layer between sheets of non-stick baking paper and pack into a freezerproof container. Defrost overnight in the fridge. Serve cold or reheat in the microwave until piping hot.

TIP:
If you don't have a cooked chicken breast, add a raw one to a pan of water and poach for 15 minutes until cooked through, before draining and shredding.

QUICK PREP

CREAMY HUNTER'S CHICKEN

⏱ **15 MINS**   🍲 **30 MINS**   ✕ **SERVES 4**

PER SERVING:
354 KCAL / 40G CARBS

SPECIAL EQUIPMENT
4 cocktail sticks

4 smoked bacon medallions
4 medium skinless, boneless
  chicken breasts (visible fat
  removed), about 130g each
low-calorie cooking spray
2 medium onions, peeled and
  thinly sliced
2 garlic cloves, peeled and
  crushed
½ medium red pepper, deseeded
  and thinly sliced
½ medium green pepper,
  deseeded and thinly sliced
1 x 400g tin chopped tomatoes
1 tbsp tomato puree
1 tbsp BBQ seasoning
¼ tsp sweet smoked paprika
1 tbsp balsamic vinegar
2 tbsp Henderson's relish (or
  Worcestershire sauce)
2 tbsp white wine vinegar
1 tbsp hot chilli sauce
1 tsp mustard powder
1 tsp white granulated
  sweetener or sugar
180g reduced-fat cream cheese

TO ACCOMPANY
50g uncooked basmati rice per
  portion, cooked according to
  packet instructions (+ 173 kcal
  per 125g cooked serving)

> **TIP:**
> Remember to remove
> the cocktail sticks before
> serving.

For this twist on the pub grub classic, we've simmered bacon-wrapped chicken in a creamy, BBQ-flavoured sauce. Smoky and mildly spicy, the sauce tastes so rich and indulgent, you'd never know it's made without using any real cream. Instead, reduced-fat cream cheese is stirred in until the sauce is velvety and luxurious. Try a portion served with some fluffy basmati rice and thank us later!

Special Occasion ────────────────

Wrap a bacon medallion around the middle of each chicken breast and secure firmly with a cocktail stick. It doesn't matter if the medallions won't wrap around the whole chicken breast and there's a gap on the underside.

Spray a large frying pan with low-calorie cooking spray and place over a medium heat. Add the onions and garlic and fry gently for about 5 minutes, until softened a little, then add the chicken breasts, red pepper and green pepper. Stir, then cook for 4–5 minutes, turning the chicken breasts over halfway through. The chicken breasts should be lightly golden.

Add the chopped tomatoes, tomato puree, BBQ seasoning, paprika, balsamic vinegar, Henderson's relish or Worcestershire sauce , white wine vinegar, hot chilli sauce, mustard powder and sweetener or sugar. Stir, then simmer, uncovered, for 10 minutes. Turn the chicken breasts over and loosely cover the pan with a lid or foil. Simmer for a further 10 minutes, or until the chicken is cooked and white throughout. Use a small sharp knife to cut into the thickest part of the chicken to check – there should be no pinkness and the juices should run clear.

Remove from the heat and stir in the cream cheese until completely blended. If the sauce is too thin, continue to simmer, uncovered, for a bit longer until the sauce has reduced and thickened to your liking. If the sauce is too thick, stir in a little water.

Remove the cocktail sticks and serve with basmati rice.

USE DF CREAM
CHEESE AND
PLANT-BASED
MILK

USE GF STOCK
CUBE AND CIDER

CIDER CHICKEN PIE

🕐 **10 MINS**   🍲 **40 MINS**   ✗ **SERVES 4**

PER SERVING:
328 KCAL /35G CARBS

SPECIAL EQUIPMENT
Large ovenproof dish
(about 18 x 27cm/7 x 10½in)

FOR THE FILLING
low-calorie cooking spray
1 small onion, peeled and thinly
  sliced
100g mushrooms, thinly sliced
3 garlic cloves, peeled and
  crushed
400g diced chicken breast
½ vegetable stock cube,
  crumbled
200ml dry apple cider
1 tbsp cornflour
100g frozen peas
3 tbsp reduced-fat cream
  cheese

FOR THE TOP
500g potatoes, peeled and cut
  into chunks
2 tbsp skimmed milk
½ tsp Dijon mustard
sea salt and freshly ground
  black pepper

TO ACCOMPANY (OPTIONAL)
80g steamed vegetables
  (+ 38 kcal per serving)

You can't beat the comfort of a homely potato-topped pie.
Combining tender chicken pieces with onions, mushrooms,
garlic and apple cider, every portion is satisfying, for just
328 calories. We've flavoured our golden-brown topping of
fluffy mash with a touch of Dijon mustard, to complement
our apple-y filling. Why not try it on your midweek menu
with a side of steamed greens?

Everyday Light ————————————————

Spray a frying pan with low-calorie cooking spray and
place over a low-medium heat. Add the onion, mushrooms
and garlic and fry for 4 minutes, until the onion is starting
to soften. Add the chicken and cook for a further 4 minutes,
until browned on all sides. Add the crumbled stock cube
then pour in the cider. Simmer gently for 8 minutes, until the
chicken is cooked through and shows no sign of pinkness.

Meanwhile, add the potatoes to a saucepan of cold, salted
water. Bring to the boil and cook for 15–20 minutes or until the
potatoes are tender. Drain well and add the milk and mustard.
Mash, taste and season with salt and pepper if needed.

Preheat the oven to 210°C (fan 190°C/gas mark 6).

Mix the cornflour with 1 tablespoon of cold water in a small
bowl until smooth. Pour into the frying pan and simmer
for a further 2 minutes until thickened slightly. Remove the
frying pan from the heat and stir in the frozen peas and
cream cheese until well blended. Season with salt and
pepper and pour the chicken mixture into the ovenproof
dish. Spoon the mashed potato over the chicken mixture,
spread it out evenly and texture the top using a fork. Bake
in the oven for 20 minutes until golden brown.

Serve with steamed vegetables or other choice of
accompaniment.

The pie will keep in the fridge for up to 3 days. To freeze,
follow standard guidelines for defrosting and reheating.

QUICK PREP

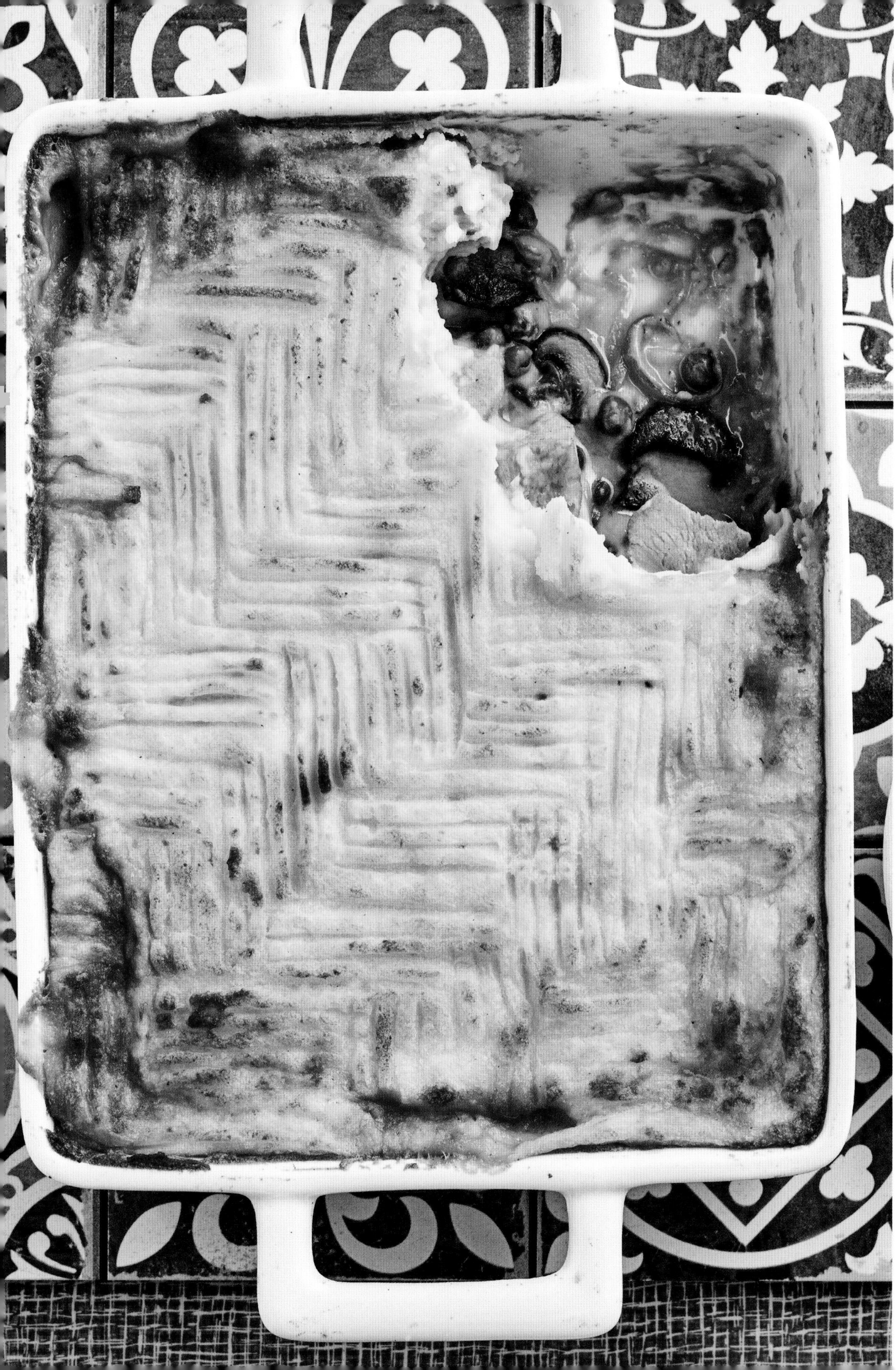

CHEESY GARLIC GAMMON

⏱ **10 MINS** 🍲 **30 MINS** ✕ **SERVES 4**

PER SERVING:
344 KCAL /9.3G CARBS

low-calorie cooking spray

2 x 250g gammon steaks (visible fat removed), cut into thin strips

1 tbsp Henderson's relish or Worcestershire sauce

1 tsp white wine vinegar

2 medium leeks, trimmed and cut into 1cm (½in)-thick slices

3 garlic cloves, peeled and crushed

200g button mushrooms, thinly sliced

1 tsp Dijon mustard

400ml chicken stock (1 chicken stock cube dissolved in 400ml boiling water)

180g reduced-fat cream cheese

60g Parmesan, finely grated

80g frozen peas

freshly ground black pepper (optional)

a few chopped chives, to garnish (optional)

TO ACCOMPANY

Creamy Mashed Potatoes from the Pinch of Nom website (+ 176 kcal per serving)

(OPTIONAL)

80g steamed vegetables (+ 38 kcal per serving)

TIP:

We recommend using a reduced-fat cream cheese rather than a fat-free one in this dish. It will be a little richer and will stand up to reheating better, if you plan to batch-cook this recipe.

Cheesy and creamy gammon – what's not to like?! We've used gammon steaks here, which are readily available, and if you're looking for new ways to serve them, look no further. The leeks, mushrooms and peas, combined with the gammon, make a delicious meal. There's no cream in sight though; we've used reduced-fat cream cheese to add the creaminess and help keep the calories down.

Special Occasion

Spray a large frying pan with low-calorie cooking spray and place over a medium heat. Add the gammon strips and seal on all sides for 3–4 minutes. Transfer the gammon strips to a plate and set aside.

If there is any liquid from the gammon in the frying pan, continue to cook it for about a minute or until it evaporates. Add the Henderson's relish and the vinegar to the frying pan, stir and scrape any meaty bits from the bottom of the pan and mix in. If needed, you can add a tablespoon or two of stock to help deglaze the pan. Continue to cook for about a minute or until most of the liquid has evaporated.

Spray the pan with low-calorie cooking spray and return to a medium heat. Add the leeks, garlic and mushrooms and cook for 5 minutes, until starting to brown, then add the mustard and cook for a minute. Add the stock and simmer, uncovered, for about 10 minutes, until reduced by half.

Remove the pan from the heat and stir in the cream cheese and Parmesan until completely blended. Place the pan over a low heat, add the gammon and simmer gently for 5–10 minutes, uncovered, until the gammon is cooked through and piping hot, and the sauce is reduced and thickened, adding the frozen peas for the last 3 minutes of cooking time.

If you find the sauce is too thick for your liking, add a little water to thin it. If it is too thin for your liking, continue to simmer to reduce further. Taste and season with black pepper if needed (you will find salt isn't needed as the gammon is naturally salty).

Sprinkle with a few chopped chives, if wished, and serve with Creamy Mashed Potatoes.

QUICK PREP

ROASTED RED PEPPER CHICKEN

🕐 **5 MINS**   🍲 **45 MINS**   ✕ **SERVES 4**

PER SERVING:
376 KCAL /27G CARBS

SPECIAL EQUIPMENT
Ovenproof dish, 28 x 20cm (11 x 8in)

low-calorie cooking spray
1 large red onion, peeled and thinly sliced
4 garlic cloves, peeled and crushed
1 x 480g jar of roasted red peppers in brine or vinegar, well drained and roughly chopped
500g passata
90g low-fat cream cheese
3 tbsp balsamic vinegar
1 tsp Worcestershire sauce or Henderson's relish
1 vegetable stock pot
½ tsp sweet smoked paprika
½ tsp dried basil
4 medium skinless chicken breasts, about 130g each
140g reduced-fat mozzarella, torn into pieces
sea salt and freshly ground black pepper
a few fresh basil leaves, to garnish

TO ACCOMPANY
75g mixed salad (+ 15 kcal per serving)

This wholesome, midweek warmer of baked chicken in a flavour-rich, roasted red pepper sauce, topped with gooey mozzarella and garnished with basil, looks almost as good as it tastes! Too delicious to eat once, you'll want to save extra portions of the freezer-friendly sauce for a rainy day (use a batch to rustle up the Creamy Roasted Red Pepper and Chicken Pasta from our website!).

Everyday Light —————————————————————

Preheat the oven to 200°C (fan 180°C/gas mark 6).

Spray a medium saucepan with low-calorie cooking spray and place over a medium heat. Add the onion, garlic and well-drained roasted red peppers and cook for about 10 minutes, or until the onion has softened and cooked through. Add the passata, cream cheese, balsamic vinegar, Worcestershire sauce or Henderson's relish, vegetable stock pot (there's no need to add water with the stock pot), sweet smoked paprika and dried basil. Stir until the stock pot has dissolved. Blitz the mixture, using a stick blender or food processor, until completely smooth. Season to taste with salt and pepper and set aside.

Spray a medium frying pan with low-calorie cooking spray and place over a medium-high heat. When the pan is hot, add the chicken breasts and cook for 2–3 minutes on each side, until golden. Place the chicken breasts in the ovenproof dish.

Spoon the sauce over the chicken breasts and scatter the torn mozzarella pieces over the top. Bake in the oven for 25-30 minutes, until the chicken is cooked through and the cheese is melted and golden. The chicken should show no sign of pinkness and the juices should run clear.

Remove from the oven, scatter over the basil leaves on top and serve with a crisp mixed salad.

The dish will keep in the fridge for up to 3 days. To freeze, follow standard guidelines for defrosting and reheating.

TIP:
The sauce can be made in bulk and frozen in portions ready for a quick dinner.

QUICK PREP

DAIRY
FREE

USE VEGAN/DF
MOZZARELLA

USE GF STOCK
CUBE

MARGHERITA COD

🕐 **10 MINS**　　🍲 **45 MINS**　　✕ **SERVES 4**

PER SERVING:
222 KCAL /8.4G CARBS

SPECIAL EQUIPMENT
Ovenproof dish, about 18 x 27cm (7 x 10½in)

low-calorie cooking spray
1 small onion, peeled and finely diced
1 x 400g tin chopped tomatoes
1 tsp garlic powder
150ml fish stock (1 fish stock cube dissolved in 150ml boiling water)
handful of fresh basil leaves, stalks removed and leaves roughly chopped
4 skinless cod loins, about 130g each
150g cherry tomatoes, halved
140g reduced-fat mozzarella, torn into pieces
freshly ground black pepper
a few extra basil leaves, stalks removed (optional)

TO ACCOMPANY
baked potato, 225g raw weight (+ 183 kcal per serving)

Sometimes the simplest flavours are the best, and that's definitely true with our Margherita Cod. Fans of our Margherita Chicken will already know what to expect! It's so fuss-free to put together – simply combine the garlicky sauce ingredients and relax while the succulent cod loins bake to flaky perfection. For a final touch of pizza-inspired magic, we've scattered juicy tomatoes and gooey mozzarella on top!

Weekly Indulgence ────────────────

Preheat the oven to 200°C (fan 180°C/gas mark 6).

Spray a small saucepan with low-calorie cooking spray and place over a medium heat. Add the onion and cook for 5–6 minutes, until softening and golden. Add the chopped tomatoes, garlic powder and stock, stir and bring to the boil. Reduce the heat and simmer gently, uncovered, for 20 minutes until the onion has softened. Stir in the chopped basil and season to taste with pepper.

Place the tomato and basil sauce in the ovenproof dish and spread it out evenly. Place the cod loins on top of the sauce, nestling them in a little but not covering them completely with the hot sauce (place the cod onto the sauce while it's still piping hot – if the sauce has cooled, the cod may not cook in the time stated). Scatter the cherry tomatoes and mozzarella over the top. Bake in the preheated oven, uncovered, for 15–20 minutes or until the cod is piping hot, opaque throughout and flakes when a knife is inserted.

Scatter a few extra basil leaves over the top, to garnish (if using), and serve with a baked potato.

The dish will keep in the fridge for up to 3 days. To freeze, follow standard guidelines for defrosting and reheating.

TIP:
It's worth using good-quality tinned chopped tomatoes to give this dish a good flavour. Some cheaper brands can be quite acidic and a little watery.

ROAST PORK AND APPLE SALAD

⏱ **20 MINS**   🍲 **NO COOK**   ✕ **SERVES 4**

PER SERVING:
199 KCAL /15G CARBS

FOR THE SALAD
100g fine green beans, trimmed
    and halved
1 green dessert apple, cored and
    cut into matchsticks
1 red dessert apple, cored and
    cut into matchsticks
2 tbsp fresh orange juice
½ small red onion, peeled and
    thinly sliced
1 medium carrot, peeled and cut
    into matchsticks
50g red cabbage, shredded
250g leftover roast pork or
    ready-cooked roast pork slices,
    cut into thin strips, all visible
    fat removed

FOR THE DRESSING
1 tbsp runny honey
2 tbsp balsamic vinegar
1 tbsp wholegrain mustard
pinch of garlic granules
sea salt and freshly ground
    black pepper

TO ACCOMPANY (OPTIONAL)
60g wholemeal bread rolls (+ 146
    kcal per roll)

A rainbow-like medley of colourful veg, tender pork strips and sliced apples, this is one of those salads that'll have you counting the minutes until lunchtime. Alongside the classic combination of pork and apple, we've tossed in beans, onion, carrot and cabbage. Whether you use roast pork leftovers or ready-cooked pork slices, our mildly tangy mustard dressing never fails to make the flavours pop!

Everyday Light ─────────────

First, prepare the salad ingredients. Bring a small saucepan of water to the boil, add the beans, cover and cook for about 1 minute, then drain and plunge into a bowl of cold water until cool. Once cool, drain the beans and set aside.

Place the cut apples in a large mixing bowl with the orange juice and toss well to coat. The orange juice will help to stop the apples turning brown.

Add the beans, onion, carrot and cabbage to the bowl, add the roast pork strips to the bowl and stir to combine.

To make the dressing, mix together the honey, balsamic vinegar, mustard and garlic granules in a small bowl and season well with salt and pepper. Add the dressing to the salad and toss to coat. Taste and add more seasoning, if needed. Serve alone with a wholemeal bread roll or as a side salad with accompaniments of your choice.

TIP:

Blanching the green beans makes them slightly more tender than if left raw. They should still retain their bright green colour and some crispness.

SNACKS AND SIDES

VEGGIE
USE A VEGGIE
STOCK POT

VEGAN
USE A VEGGIE
STOCK POT

FREEZE ME

BATCH COOK

DAIRY FREE

GLUTEN FREE

BOULANGERE POTATOES

🕐 **15 MINS**   🍲 **1 HOUR 30 MINS**   ✕ **SERVES 4**

PER SERVING:
211 KCAL /42G CARBS

SPECIAL EQUIPMENT
Ovenproof dish, about 28 x 24cm (11 x 9½in), mandoline (useful but not essential)

2 tbsp white wine vinegar
1 tsp garlic powder or granules
150ml chicken or vegetable stock (1 chicken or vegetable stock pot dissolved in 150ml boiling water)
800g potatoes, thinly sliced (peeled if you like)
2 onions, peeled and thinly sliced
low-calorie cooking spray
sea salt and freshly ground black pepper

Our Boulangere Potatoes have all the luxury of dauphinoise potatoes, for a fraction of the calories! Made with a short list of simple ingredients, they make for a tasty break from mash or roasties with meat or fish. We've built layers of flavour with thinly sliced potatoes and onions, and baked them to perfection in rich, garlicky stock.

Weekly Indulgence —————————————

Preheat the oven to 210°C (fan 190°C/gas mark 6).

Mix the vinegar and garlic powder into the stock and pour half into the bottom of the ovenproof dish.

Layer potato slices across the bottom of the dish. Scatter some onion slices over and repeat. You should have about 3 layers at the end. Pour over the rest of the stock and tightly cover with foil. Place into the oven and bake for 1 hour.

Remove from the oven and take off the foil. Spray the top with low-calorie cooking spray and place back into the oven for 30 minutes.

Season with salt and pepper and serve with a main of your choice.

The dish will keep in the fridge for up to 3 days. To freeze, cool as quickly as possible and divide into individual portions. Freeze in individual freezerproof containers. Defrost overnight in the fridge, cover with foil and reheat in the oven at 210°C (fan 190°C/gas mark 6) until piping hot.

TIPS:

If you have a mandoline or a food processor with a slicing attachment, it will make quick work of the prep for this dish! If not, make sure your knife is super sharp and cut thin slices. While there's no need to peel the potatoes, you can if you wish. This dish is really tasty with a tablespoon (5g) of finely grated Parmesan over the top at the end too! Just add 20 kcal per portion.

QUICK PREP

VEGGIE

FREEZE ME

BATCH COOK

DAIRY FREE

LOW CARB

GLUTEN FREE

SWEET POTATO HASH BROWNS

🕐 **10 MINS**   🍲 **40 MINS**   ✕ **MAKES 8**

PER HASH BROWN:
56 KCAL / 9.7G CARBS

SPECIAL EQUIPMENT
8cm (3¼in) plain round
biscuit cutter (useful but not
essential)

300g sweet potato, peeled and
   coarsely grated
2 spring onions, trimmed and
   thinly sliced
2 tsp cornflour
1 tsp garlic granules
1 tsp onion powder
½ tsp smoked paprika
½ tsp salt
pinch of freshly ground black
   pepper
1 medium egg, beaten
low-calorie cooking spray
1 tbsp finely chopped fresh
   chives, to serve

TO ACCOMPANY (OPTIONAL)
medium fried eggs
   (+ 82 kcal per egg)

Have you ever tried hash browns with a sweet potato twist? Just as crispy and satisfying as more calorie-laden versions, you'll only need basic ingredients and a handful of store-cupboard spices to put these together. Use them to take your favourite cooked breakfast to the next level, with a moreish, sweet potato crunch. Not bad for 55 calories each!

Everyday Light ———————————————

Preheat the oven to 200°C (fan 180°C/gas mark 6) and line a baking tray with non-stick baking paper.

Place the grated sweet potato into a bowl with the spring onions, cornflour, garlic granules, onion powder, paprika, salt and pepper. Add the beaten egg a little at a time and mix until the mixture is well coated and sticky. (You may not need to add all the egg.) The mixture should be stiff enough to shape into a hash brown.

You can shape the mixture into your desired hash brown shape; we shaped the potato mixture using an 8cm (3¼in) plain round biscuit cutter. Press the potato inside the cutter and compact it into shape. Remove the cutter and repeat with the remaining mixture to make 8 hash browns.

Place on the lined baking tray and spray with some low-calorie cooking spray. Bake in the oven for 20 minutes.

After 20 minutes, flip the hash browns. Spray with more low-calorie cooking spray and cook for a further 20 minutes until golden and crisp.

Sprinkle with chives and serve with a fried egg, your choice of accompaniment, or alongside a cooked breakfast!

The hash browns will keep in the fridge in an airtight container for up to 3 days. To freeze the hash browns, cool as quickly as possible. Layer between sheets of non-stick baking paper and pack into a freezerproof container. Defrost in the fridge overnight and reheat in the oven at 200°C (fan 180°C/gas mark 6) until piping hot.

QUICK PREP

SWEET CARROT AND GINGER SLAW

🕐 **10 MINS**   🗑 **NO COOK**   ✕ **SERVES 2**

* PLUS 20 MINS MARINATING

PER SERVING:
69 KCAL /13G CARBS

SPECIAL EQUIPMENT
Vegetable peeler, fine grater

1 tbsp clear honey
2 tbsp rice vinegar
1 tsp peeled and finely grated
   root ginger
pinch of salt
2 medium carrots, peeled
a few snipped chives

This versatile slaw makes for a really tasty salad or side dish. Add some crunch to a buffet or burger night with these ribbons of fresh carrot, dressed in a sweet honey and ginger-infused vinegar. There's no need to cook anything, just set your slaw aside for 20 minutes to let all the flavours mingle together.

Everyday Light ─────────────────────

In a bowl, mix the honey, vinegar and ginger with the salt.

Using a vegetable peeler, cut the carrots into thin ribbons. Add the carrot ribbons to the dressing and toss until well coated. Cover and allow to marinate for 20 minutes to allow the flavours to mix.

Sprinkle with snipped chives and serve.

QUICK PREP

DAIRY FREE

USE DF/VEGAN FETA

LOW CARB

GLUTEN FREE

PRAWN SAGANAKI

🕐 **10 MINS**　　🍲 **25 MINS**　　✕ **SERVES 4**

PER SERVING:
208 KCAL / 8.4G CARBS

SPECIAL EQUIPMENT
Large ovenproof dish (about 18 x 27cm/7 x 10½in) or 4 small individual ovenproof dishes (about 10 x 14cm/4 x 5½in)

1 x 400g tin chopped tomatoes
2 garlic cloves, peeled and finely chopped
1 tbsp tomato puree
1 tsp fresh thyme, stalks removed and leaves finely chopped
1 tsp fresh oregano, stalks removed and leaves finely chopped.
small pinch of dried chilli flakes
200g reduced-fat feta, cut into 3cm (1¼in) cubes
200g cherry tomatoes, halved
2 tsp capers, drained
low-calorie cooking spray
300g frozen raw king prawns, defrosted and well-drained
freshly ground black pepper, to taste

TO ACCOMPANY
60g wholemeal bread rolls
(+ 146 kcal per roll)

Nothing says 'Greek beachside taverna' quite like our Prawn Saganaki. To recreate the flavours you'd find on a sunny Mediterranean holiday, we've baked our prawns in a rich, chilli-infused tomato sauce and topped it all off with crumbly feta. With fresh thyme, oregano and capers stirred in, you'll definitely want to wipe your dish clean with a crusty wholemeal bread roll. Don't be afraid to add extra chilli flakes, if you're feeling brave!

Weekly Indulgence ─────────────

Preheat the oven to 200°C (fan 180°C/gas mark 6). Put the tinned tomatoes, garlic, tomato puree, half of the thyme, half of the oregano and the chilli flakes in a mixing bowl. Season with pepper and stir well.

Tip the mixture into the ovenproof dish or divide between 4 individual ovenproof dishes. Spread the mixture out evenly. Scatter the feta, cherry tomatoes and capers over the tomato mixture. Sprinkle with the remaining thyme and oregano, season with more pepper and spray with a little low-calorie cooking spray.

Bake in the oven for 10 minutes until the tomato sauce is starting to bubble. Remove from the oven and add the raw prawns, poking them down into the sauce among the tomatoes and feta. Return to the oven and bake for a further 10–15 minutes until the prawns are cooked through. The prawns should no longer be grey but should be pink on the outside and white inside. The feta should be starting to turn golden brown around the edges and softening in the middle.

Serve at once with wholemeal bread rolls to mop up the juices.

TIP:
There's no need to season with salt as the feta is already salty. If you'd like to make this dish more authentic, you can add a tablespoon or two of Ouzo to the tomato mixture, but remember to adjust the calories accordingly.

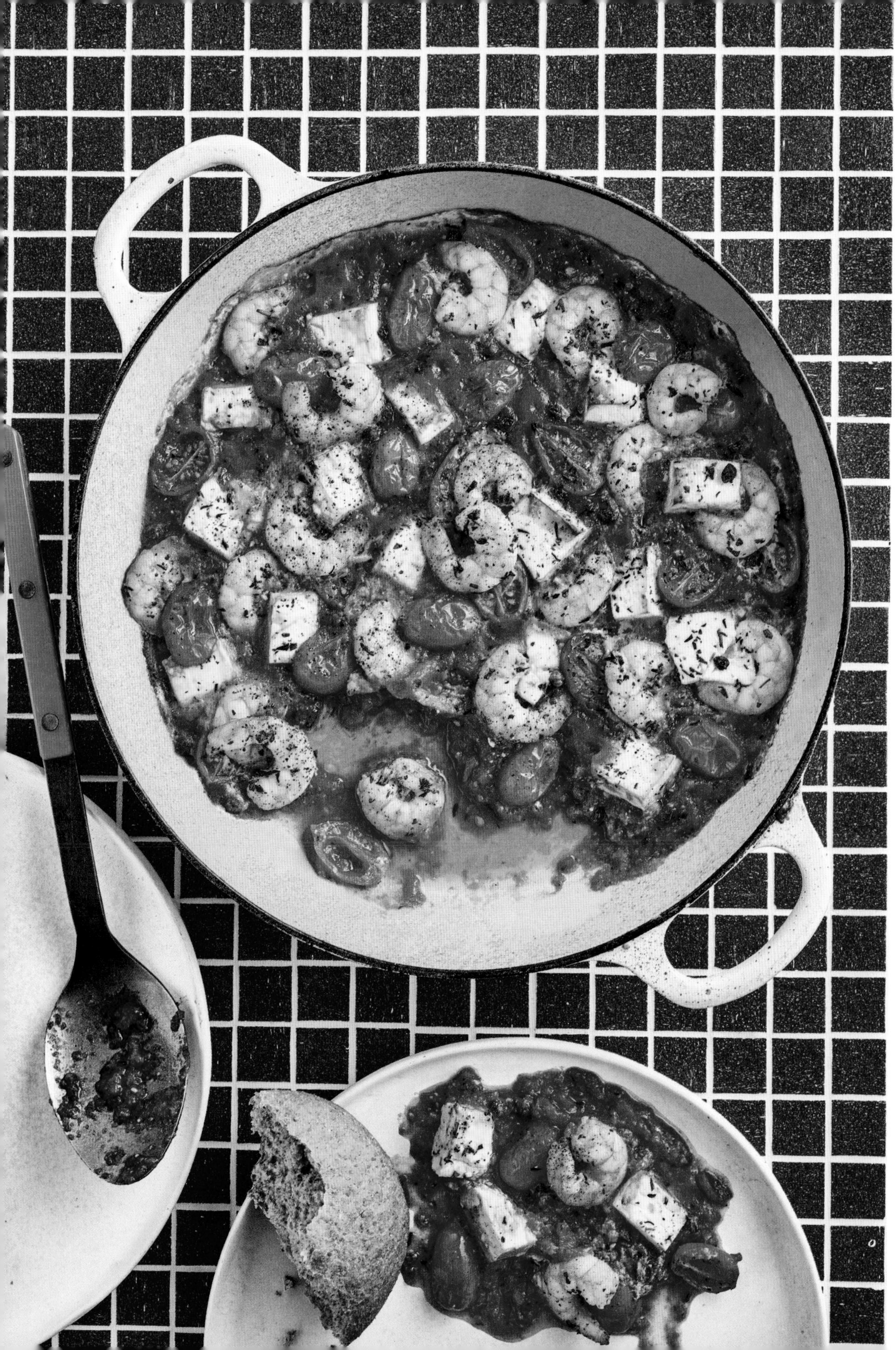

VEGGIE

FREEZE ME

BATCH COOK

DAIRY FREE

USE DF REDUCED-FAT SPREAD

GLUTEN FREE

USE GF FLOUR AND OATS

WINTER BERRY COBBLER

🕐 **10 MINS**　　🍲 **45 MINS**　　✕ **SERVES 6**

PER PORTION:
270 KCAL / 51G CARBS

SPECIAL EQUIPMENT
18 x 27cm (7 x 10½in)
ovenproof dish

400g frozen cranberries
400g cooking apples, peeled, cored and thinly sliced
2 large oranges, peeled, segmented, and all membrane and pith removed
finely grated zest of 1 large orange
120g white granulated sweetener
1 tbsp cornflour
80g plain flour
pinch of salt
30g reduced-fat spread
40g rolled oats
2 medium eggs, beaten

TO ACCOMPANY (OPTIONAL)
A swirl of reduced-fat aerosol cream (+ 24 kcal per serving)

American in origin, a cobbler is similar to a fruit crumble, with a golden, crunchy topping baked over a generous layer of sweetened fruits. A twist on our Summer Berry Cobbler recipe, this one uses juicy winter fruits: cranberries, apples and oranges. The fruit will get soft and syrupy as it bakes, so make sure you leave a few gaps in your cobbler for that lovely syrup to bubble through. Top it with a swirl of aerosol cream and you're in for a real treat!

Weekly Indulgence ─────────────

Preheat the oven to 210°C (fan 190°C/gas mark 6).

Place the frozen cranberries, sliced apple, orange and orange zest in an ovenproof dish. Sprinkle over 100g of the sweetener (save 20g for later use) and cornflour and mix well. Spread the fruit out evenly.

Place the flour, remaining 20g sweetener, salt and reduced-fat spread in a mixing bowl and, using your fingers, rub together until it resembles fine breadcrumbs. Stir in the oats, then add the eggs and mix until combined.

Use a tablespoon to place spoonfuls of the mixture onto the fruit, leaving gaps for the fruit to bubble through. Bake in the oven for 25 minutes, until the top is lightly golden.

Remove from the oven, cover the top loosely with a sheet of foil, then return to the oven for a further 20 minutes, until the apples are tender, the fruit is bubbling, and the top is golden brown. Serve warm, alone or with aerosol cream.

The cobber will keep in the fridge for up to 2–3 days. If you want to freeze the cobbler, freeze it in portions to make it easy to reheat in individual servings. Defrost in the fridge, then reheat (loosely covered) in the microwave for 2–3 minutes or until piping hot.

QUICK PREP

TIP:
Make sure to slice the apples thinly so that they cook in the time stated.

BISCOFF SPONGE TRAYBAKE

🕐 **10 MINS**   🍲 **25 MINS**   ✕ **MAKES 16 SQUARES**

PER SQUARE:
127 KCAL /14G CARBS

SPECIAL EQUIPMENT
20 x 22cm (8 x 8½in)
ovenproof dish

100g reduced-fat spread, plus a little extra for greasing
100g self-raising flour
50g white granulated sweetener
50g caster sugar
½ tsp baking powder
2 medium eggs
1 tsp vanilla extract
¼ tsp ground cinnamon
50g smooth Biscoff spread

FOR THE TOPPING
30g smooth Biscoff spread

These moreish little squares of Biscoff sponge are light, moist and topped with a layer of creamy Biscoff spread for a little extra indulgence. They have a caramel, biscuity flavour with a little cinnamon to add a hint of warming spice and are perfect with a cuppa. These are so quick and easy to make they're sure to become a family favourite!

Everyday Light ────────────────

Preheat the oven to 180°C (fan 160°C/gas mark 4) and grease the ovenproof dish well with the extra reduced-fat spread.

Put the flour, reduced-fat spread, granulated sweetener, caster sugar, baking powder, eggs, vanilla extract, cinnamon and 50g Biscoff spread in a medium mixing bowl and beat for 1–2 minutes with an electric whisk, until light and creamy. Alternatively, you can use a wooden spoon, but it will take more effort.

Use a rubber spatula to scrape the mixture from the mixing bowl into the greased ovenproof dish and level the surface with a knife.

Bake for 20–25 minutes, until risen and golden all over. To test if the sponge is ready, insert a small sharp knife into the centre. When the sponge is cooked the knife will come out clean. Leave the sponge in the dish to cool.

Spread the Biscoff spread evenly over the top of the cooled sponge in a thin layer, texture it with a round bladed knife and cut into 16 squares.

The traybake will keep in an airtight container in the fridge for up to 3 days, or can be frozen after decorating. Place in a single layer in a suitable freezerproof container or layer between sheets of non-stick baking paper. Defrost at room temperature.

TIP:
Make sure to use white granulated sweetener that has the same texture and weight as sugar.

VEGGIE

VEGAN

USE VEGAN
SPREAD

FREEZE
ME

BATCH
COOK

DAIRY
FREE

USE DF SPREAD

ORANGE AND GINGER RHUBARB CRUMBLE

🕐 **15 MINS**   🍲 **55 MINS**   ✕ **SERVES 6**

PER SERVING:
289 KCAL / 46G CARBS

SPECIAL EQUIPMENT
18 x 27cm (7 x 10½in)
ovenproof dish

900g fresh rhubarb, trimmed
  and cut into 3cm (1¼in) lengths
6 tbsp white granulated
  sweetener
½ tsp ground ginger
finely grated zest and juice of
  1 large orange

FOR THE CRUMBLE TOPPING
150g plain flour
75g reduced-fat spread
50g rolled porridge oats
2 tbsp white granulated
  sweetener
½ tsp ground ginger

TO ACCOMPANY (OPTIONAL)
¼ tin (100g) light custard
  (+ 79 kcal per serving)

This Orange and Ginger Rhubarb Crumble is a wholesome hug in a bowl! Filled with a lightly-spiced combo of zesty orange, punchy ginger and rhubarb, it goes together too well not to eat again and again. It's a good job that it's super simple to prepare, slimming-friendly topping of crunchy, oven-baked oats included. Bring on the custard!

Weekly Indulgence

Preheat the oven to 200°C (fan 180°C/gas mark 6).

Put the rhubarb in a medium saucepan with the sweetener, ground ginger, orange zest and orange juice. Stir to combine. Cover, place over a low heat and simmer gently for about 20 minutes, or until the rhubarb is soft when a sharp knife is inserted and most of the pieces are still holding their shape.

Taste the rhubarb mixture and add a little more sweetener if needed, to suit your own taste. Transfer the mixture into the ovenproof dish and spread out evenly.

Put the flour in a medium mixing bowl. Add the reduced-fat spread and rub it in, using your fingers, until the mixture resembles coarse breadcrumbs. Stir in the oats, sweetener and ground ginger until evenly mixed, then sprinkle evenly over the rhubarb mixture.

Place on a baking tray and bake in the oven for 30–35 minutes, until the crumble topping is golden brown and the rhubarb is soft.

Serve hot with a glug of custard or other accompaniment of your choice.

TIP:
This crumble is lightly spiced with ginger – just add a little more if you'd prefer a stronger ginger flavour!

QUICK PREP

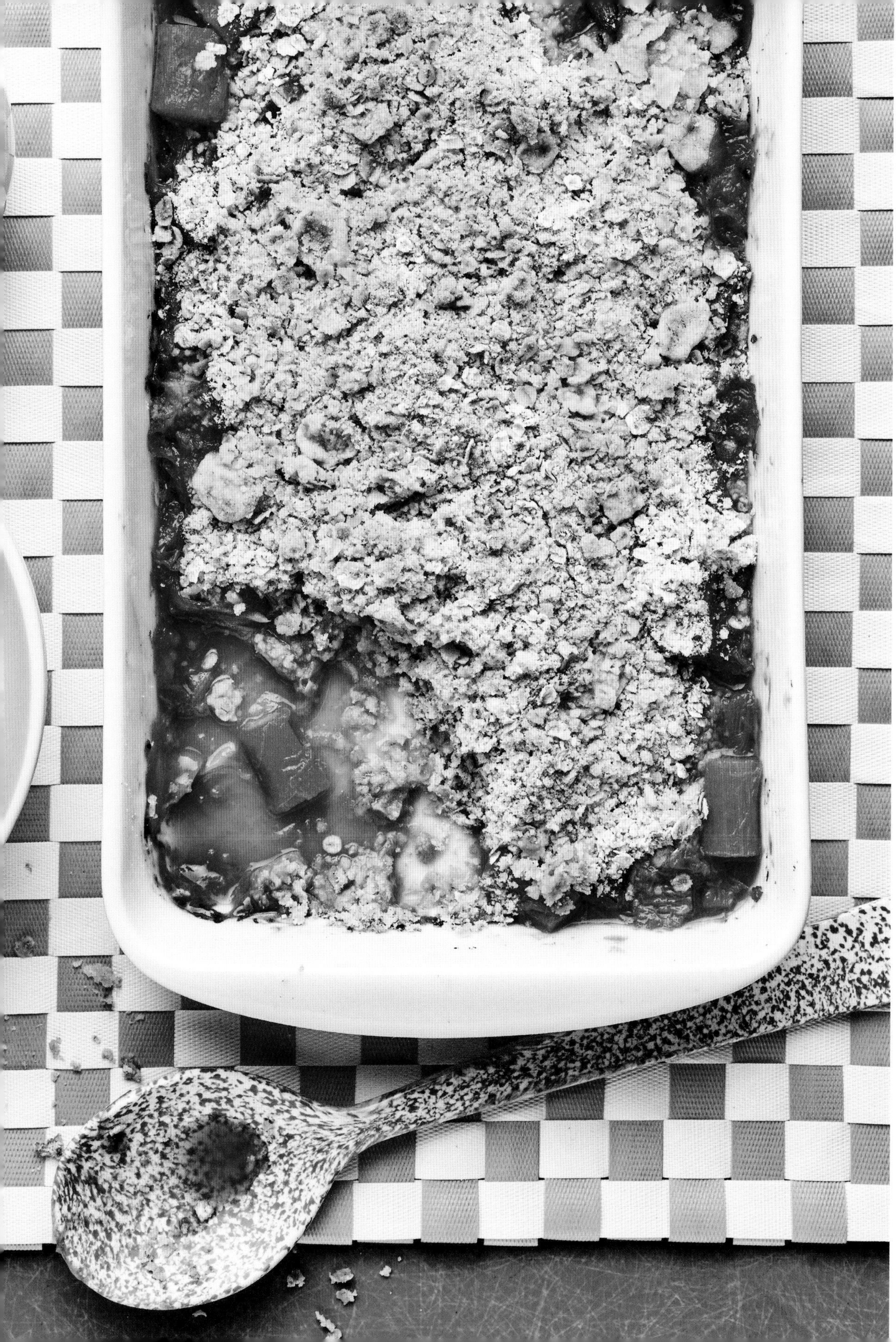

CARAMEL APPLE UPSIDE-DOWN CAKE

🕐 **10 MINS**　　🍲 **45 MINS**　　✕ **SERVES 8**

* PLUS 5 MINS RESTING

PER SERVING:
229 KCAL / 29G CARBS

SPECIAL EQUIPMENT
Round, deep non-stick 18cm (7in) cake tin

2 tbsp low-calorie caramel syrup (we use Sweet Freedom)
2 dessert apples, peeled, cored and thinly sliced

FOR THE CAKE
100g reduced-fat spread, plus a little extra for greasing
100g self-raising flour
50g white granulated sweetener
50g caster sugar
½ tsp baking powder
½ tsp ground cinnamon
2 medium eggs
1 tsp vanilla extract

TO ACCOMPANY (OPTIONAL)
¼ tin (100g) light custard (+ 79 kcal per serving)

Caramelised apples work together beautifully in this topsy-turvy cake. Using low-calorie syrup to bring the calories down, we've coated our layer of apple slices in a sticky, caramel-flavoured glaze. Bake the lightly spiced cinnamon sponge until it's fluffy and gorgeously golden. Enjoy it (right-side up!) with a cuppa, a glug of custard or both!

Weekly Indulgence ──────────────

Preheat the oven to 180°C (fan 160°C/gas mark 4) and grease the base and sides of the cake tin well with the little extra reduced-fat spread. Line the base of the tin with a disc of non-stick baking paper.

Pour the low-calorie caramel syrup into the base of the tin and spread it out evenly. Arrange the apple slices on top of the syrup, overlapping them to form a ring around the edge of the tin. Arrange overlapping apple slices in the space in the centre.

Put the flour, reduced-fat spread, granulated sweetener, caster sugar, baking powder, cinnamon, eggs and vanilla extract in a medium mixing bowl and beat together for 1–2 minutes with an electric hand whisk until light and creamy. Alternatively, you can use a wooden spoon, but it will take more effort.

Use a rubber spatula to scrape the mixture from the mixing bowl on top of the apple slices in the cake tin. Level the surface with a knife. Bake in the oven for 45 minutes, or until risen and golden brown all over. To test if it's ready, insert a small sharp knife or skewer into the centre of the sponge. When the cake is cooked, the knife will come out clean.

Remove from the oven and leave to sit for about 5 minutes. Run a round-bladed knife around the sponge to loosen it from the tin. Turn out onto a serving plate and remove the non-stick baking paper disc. Cut into 8 slices and serve hot or cold, alone or with custard.

The cake will keep in the fridge for up to 3 days. To freeze, follow standard guidelines for defrosting and reheating.

TIPS:

Use a white granulated sweetener that has the same weight, texture and sweetness as sugar. It's important to use a deep tin as the cake will rise up and over the top of a shallow tin.

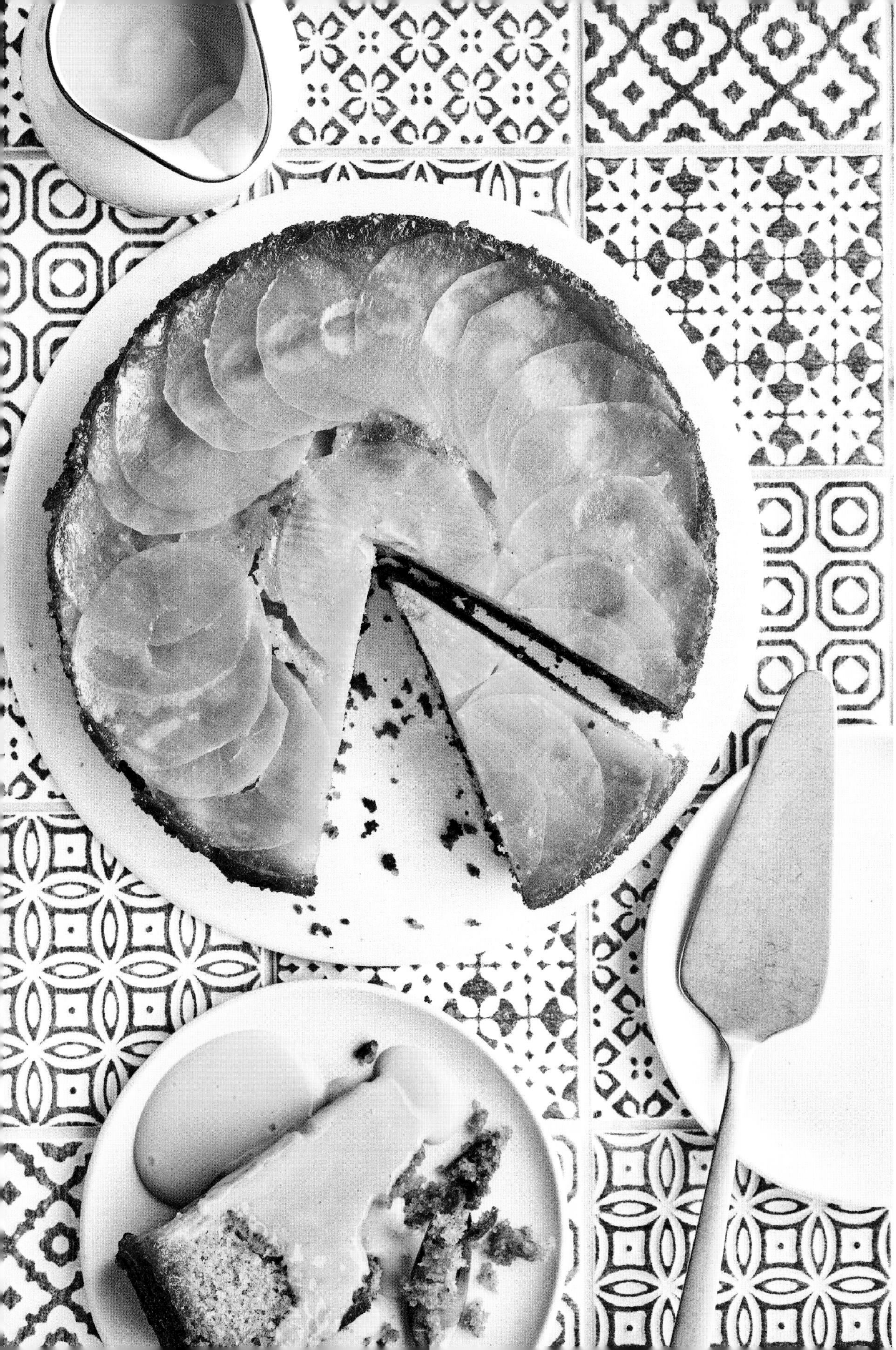

VEGGIE

GLUTEN FREE

USE GF OREO BISCUITS

COOKIES AND CREAM CHEESECAKE

🕐 **15 MINS**　　🍲 **1 HOUR**　　✕ **SERVES 8**

* PLUS 1 HOUR COOLING AND MINIMUM OF 2 HOURS CHILLING

PER PORTION:
266 KCAL /28G CARBS

SPECIAL EQUIPMENT
20cm (8in) round, loose-bottomed cake tin

FOR THE BASE
30g reduced-fat spread, melted, plus a little extra, unmelted, for greasing
215g Oreo biscuits

FOR THE FILLING
300g low-fat cream cheese
300g fat-free Greek-style yoghurt
1 tbsp white granulated sweetener
1 tsp vanilla extract
2 tbsp cornflour
2 medium eggs

FOR THE TOP
1 tbsp low-calorie chocolate syrup
1 Oreo biscuit, crushed

Oreo fans, listen up – this oh-so-creamy cheesecake recipe is for you! Using fat-free yoghurt and low-fat cream cheese, we've managed to make this delightful, velvety bake without a pot of cream in sight. You only need two ingredients to make the crunchy base (crushed-up Oreo biscuits and reduced-fat spread). If you're looking for a guaranteed showstopper, this is the one!

Weekly Indulgence

Preheat the oven to 160°C (fan 140°C/gas mark 3), grease the cake tin with the unmelted reduced-fat spread and line the base with non-stick baking paper.

Put the Oreo biscuits for the base in a food processor and blitz until they resemble fine breadcrumbs. Tip 175g of the biscuit crumbs into a mixing bowl, add the melted reduced-fat spread and mix well. Press the biscuit mixture into the base of the prepared tin and place in the fridge to chill while you make the filling.

Put the cream cheese, Greek yoghurt, sweetener, vanilla extract, cornflour and eggs in a large mixing bowl and beat with a balloon whisk or wooden spoon until well combined. Fold in the remaining 40g biscuit crumbs. Transfer the filling mixture onto the chilled biscuit base and place the tin on a baking tray. Place on a low shelf in the oven and bake for 50–60 minutes, until it's set around the edges but still has a wobble in the centre.

Remove from the oven and leave to cool for 1 hour. Once cooled, place in the fridge to chill for a minimum of 2 hours but it's best left to chill overnight.

Remove the cheesecake from the tin, peel away the baking paper and place onto your serving plate.

Drizzle over the low-calorie chocolate syrup and sprinkle the crushed Oreo biscuit over the top. Slice into 8 and serve!

VEGGIE

FREEZE ME

WITHOUT THE FROSTING

BATCH COOK

DAIRY FREE

USE DF CREAM CHEESE AND SPREAD

GLUTEN FREE

USE GF FLOUR AND BAKING POWDER

CHOCOLATE SPONGE TRAYBAKE

🕐 **10 MINS**   🍲 **25 MINS**   ✕ **MAKES 16 SQUARES**

* **PLUS 45–60 MINS COOLING**

PER SQUARE:
111 KCAL /13G CARBS

SPECIAL EQUIPMENT
20 x 22cm (8 x 8½in)
ovenproof dish

100g reduced-fat spread, plus
   a little extra for greasing
100g self-raising flour
50g white granulated sweetener
50g caster sugar
½ tsp baking powder
15g cocoa powder
2 medium eggs
1 tsp vanilla extract

FOR THE FROSTING
10g cocoa powder
25g white granulated sweetener
2 tbsp cold water
125g reduced-fat cream cheese

These spongy little squares don't look or taste slimming friendly, and yet they're nice and light at 111 calories each! For our creamy chocolate frosting, we've used a lower-calorie combination of reduced-fat cream cheese, sweetener and cocoa powder. They're easy to rustle up from scratch, and you can always keep a batch handy in the fridge or freezer for a sweet treat at a moment's notice.

Everyday Light

Preheat the oven to 180°C (fan 160°C/gas mark 4) and grease the ovenproof dish well with the little extra reduced-fat spread.

Put the flour, reduced-fat spread, granulated sweetener, caster sugar, baking powder, cocoa powder, eggs and vanilla extract in a medium mixing bowl and beat together for 1–2 minutes with an electric whisk until light and creamy. Alternatively, you can use a wooden spoon, but it will take more effort.

Use a rubber spatula to scrape the mixture from the mixing bowl into the greased ovenproof dish and level the surface with a knife. Bake in the oven for 20–25 minutes, until risen and spongy. To test if the sponge is ready, insert a small sharp knife into the centre; when the sponge is cooked the knife will come out clean. Leave the sponge in the dish to cool. At this point the sponge can be frozen, then defrosted at room temperature before icing.

Put the cocoa powder, white granulated sweetener and water in a small saucepan and stir with a wooden spoon until smooth. Place over a low heat and bring to a gentle simmer. Simmer gently for 1–2 minutes, stirring until smooth, glossy and the consistency of melted chocolate. Using a spatula, scrape into a small bowl and leave until just cool.

Put the cream cheese in a medium bowl and mix with a wooden spoon until softened and smooth. Add the cocoa mixture and stir until evenly combined. Spread the chocolate frosting evenly over the top of the cooled sponge, texture it with a round-bladed knife and cut into 16 squares.

TIP:

Make sure to use white granulated sweetener with the same texture and weight as sugar.

MINT CHOCOLATE MOUSSE

🕐 **10 MINS**   🍲 **NO COOK**   ✕ **SERVES 6**

* PLUS MINIMUM 2 HOURS CHILLING

PER SERVING:
148 KCAL /6.5G CARBS

SPECIAL EQUIPMENT
Electric hand whisk, 6 x 125ml ramekin dishes

270ml light double cream
  alternative
2 x 11g low-calorie instant
  choc mint hot chocolate
  powder sachets
½ tsp vegan gelatine powder
a few drops of peppermint
  essence
30g milk chocolate chips
a few fresh mint leaves,
  to decorate

Pudding recipes don't come easier than this! Our light, airy chocolate mousse takes just 10 minutes to prepare and a couple of hours in the fridge to chill. By combining a half-fat alternative to double cream with sachets of hot chocolate powder, we've said goodbye to lots of calories and hello to minty, chocolate-y flavour. A lovely end to any meal, there are less than 150 calories in each dreamy little pot.

Everyday Light

Place the light double cream alternative, instant choc mint hot chocolate powder, vegan gelatine powder and a few drops of peppermint essence into a large bowl. Whisk using an electric hand whisk until it is thick and has doubled in volume.

Fold in the chocolate chips, reserving a few for decoration, and divide among the 6 ramekins. Sprinkle on the reserved chocolate chips.

Cover and chill for a minimum of 2 hours.

Decorate with mint leaves before serving, and enjoy.

SWEET TREATS

217

VEGGIE

CHOCOLATE AND GINGER TART

⏱ **20 MINS** 🍲 **40 MINS** ✕ **SERVES 8**

* PLUS 1 HOUR COOLING AND A MINIMUM OF 2 HOURS CHILLING

PER SERVING:
314 KCAL /44G CARBS

SPECIAL EQUIPMENT
24cm (9½in) loose-bottomed tart tin, food processor (useful but not essential)

FOR THE TART CASE
25g reduced-fat spread, melted, plus a little extra, unmelted, for greasing
250g ginger nut biscuits
1 medium egg white

FOR THE FILLING
400ml skimmed milk
4 medium egg yolks
50g caster sugar
50g white granulated sweetener
15g cocoa powder
30g cornflour
40g dark chocolate, broken into pieces

TO DECORATE
2 tsp cocoa powder
edible gold and silver leaf, or gold and silver sugar sprinkles

TO ACCOMPANY (OPTIONAL)
12.5g average portion reduced-fat aerosol cream (+ 24 kcal per serving)

> **TIP:**
> Use white granulated sweetener that has the same texture, sweetness and weight as sugar; not the powdered type.

We've turned crushed-up ginger nut biscuits into a crisp tart case, with a flavour that brings out the best from the velvety chocolate filling. Baked and then chilled until it has the consistency of a set custard, this is worthy of a dinner party dessert – no one will ever guess it's so slimming friendly.

Special Occasion ─────────────

Preheat the oven to 200°C (fan 180°C/gas mark 6) and grease the tart tin with a little reduced-fat spread.

Put the biscuits in a large, strong food bag, seal and bash with a rolling pin into a very fine crumb.

Add the egg white to a clean mixing bowl and beat with an electric whisk until frothy and slightly thickened. Add the crushed biscuits, along with the melted reduced-fat spread, and mix until combined. Scrape the mixture into the tart tin. Using the back of a spoon, press the crumb mixture down onto the base and up the sides of the tin to form a biscuit crumb tart case. Place the tart tin onto a baking tray and bake for 10 minutes until the case is crisp. Remove from the oven and lower the oven temperature to 180°C (fan 160°C/gas mark 4).

Put the milk, egg yolks, caster sugar, granulated sweetener, cocoa powder and cornflour in a small saucepan and whisk until smooth. Set the pan over a low heat and whisk continually while heating for 5–8 minutes, until the mixture has thickened. It should coat the back of a spoon. Remove the pan from the heat and add the chocolate. Whisk until melted. The mixture should be smooth and glossy.

Pour the filling mixture into the tart case and spread it out evenly with the back of a spoon. Bake for 20 minutes. The top of the chocolate tart should have a matte finish and be set, with a slight wobble when you shake the tin.

Remove from the oven and leave to cool for 1 hour, then place into the fridge to chill for a minimum of 2 hours. When chilled, you can decorate the top. Slice the tart into 8 portions and serve!

RASPBERRY SORBET

🕐 **10 MINS**　🗑 **NO COOK**　✕ **SERVES 4**

* PLUS 4 HOURS FREEZING

PER SERVING:
104 KCAL /17G CARBS

SPECIAL EQUIPMENT
1-litre freezerproof container

500g frozen raspberries
4 tbsp low-calorie fruit syrup
　(we use Sweet Freedom)
juice of 1 lemon

We've used a low-calorie syrup to rustle up this fruity frozen treat in a fraction of the time it usually takes to make your own sorbet. The result is a soft, smooth, sweet sorbet that doesn't need churning to help it set. Turn raspberries, syrup and a squeeze of lemon juice into a refreshing, light treat that's delicious served after just about any meal.

Everyday Light ————————————————

Remove the raspberries from the freezer and leave to soften slightly in their bag for 10 minutes.

Place the raspberries, low-calorie fruit syrup and lemon juice in a food processor or blender and blitz until thick and smooth. You will need to scrape the mixture down from the side of the food processor occasionally. You may need to do this in several batches depending on the size of your food processor or blender.

Place a sieve over a medium mixing bowl. Working quickly, add some of the soft sorbet and push through the sieve and into the bowl using a wooden spoon to remove and discard the raspberry seeds. Make sure to scrape all the sorbet off the bottom of the sieve and into the bowl. You will find it easier to do this in several batches.

Quickly scrape the soft sorbet into the freezerproof container and roughly spread it out. Cover with a lid and place in the freezer for about 4 hours or until frozen.

When ready to serve, remove from the freezer and leave to soften for 10–15 minutes before scooping into small dishes.

QUICK PREP

VEGGIE

FREEZE ME

BATCH COOK

GLUTEN FREE

SALTED CARAMEL FROYO

🕐 **15 MINS**　　🍲 **NO COOK**　　✕ **SERVES 8**

* PLUS 8 HOURS FREEZING

PER SERVING:
146 KCAL / 21G CARBS

SPECIAL EQUIPMENT
2-litre freezerproof container

1kg fat-free thick Greek yoghurt
6 tbsp caramel syrup alternative
　fruit syrup (we use Sweet
　Freedom)
3 tsp caramel flavouring
80g sugar-free butter candies
　(we use Werther's Original
　Sugar-Free Butter Candies)
1 tsp sea salt flakes

You'll never regret keeping smooth, scoop-ready portions of our Salted Caramel Froyo on standby! Ready to freeze in 15 minutes, it'll curb your sweet cravings without a pot of cream in sight. To lower the calories without spoiling the fun, we've used crushed sugar-free hard butter candies to give our luscious caramel-flavoured fat-free yoghurt blend an irresistible crunch.

Everyday Light ———————————————

Place the yoghurt in a medium mixing bowl and stir until smooth. Using a large metal spoon, fold in the caramel syrup and caramel flavouring until evenly mixed.

Scrape into the freezerproof container and spread out evenly. Cover with a lid and place in the freezer for about 4 hours, or until solid.

Meanwhile, place the butter candies in a strong food bag. Seal the bag, then place inside another strong food bag and seal. Place on the work surface and bash with a rolling pin until the butter candies are crushed into a mixture of fine, powdery pieces and small chunks. Set aside.

After about 4 hours, remove the frozen yoghurt mixture from the freezer and leave for about 15 minutes, or until softened a little. Scoop out slightly-softened chunks and place in a food processor or blender. You will probably need to do this in several batches, depending on the capacity of your appliance.

Blitz the slightly softened chunks of yoghurt mixture until smooth and creamy, then place in a medium mixing bowl. Working quickly, repeat with the remaining chunks. Add the crushed butter candies and sea salt to the blitzed frozen yoghurt mixture in the bowl. Working quickly, fold in using a large metal spoon until evenly combined. Don't allow the mixture to melt; it should still be semi frozen. Scrape back into the freezerproof container and spread out. Cover with a lid and place in the freezer for about 4 hours, or until frozen throughout.

Remove from the freezer for about 15 minutes to soften a little before serving.

TIP:
Before starting, make sure you have room in your freezer for the freezerproof container you are using.

QUICK PREP

LEMON AND LIME POTS

🕐 **10 MINS**   🍲 **NO COOK**   ✕ **MAKES 4 POTS**

* PLUS MINIMUM 30 MINS CHILLING

PER POT:
159 KCAL /27G CARBS

SPECIAL EQUIPMENT
4 x 125ml ramekin dishes
(preferably glass)

80g lemon and lime
   fine-cut marmalade
100g low-fat cream cheese
60g lemon curd
200g fat-free Greek-style
   yoghurt

TO SERVE
1 gingernut biscuit, crushed
slice of lemon or lime, quartered

TO ACCOMPANY (OPTIONAL)
Churros (see Pinch of Nom
   website for recipe) (+ 23 kcal
   per churro) or crisp biscuit of
   your choice.

Sometimes you need something light yet sweet to finish off your meal, and these citrusy little desserts are just the ticket. We've topped a layer of zingy lemon and lime marmalade with a velvety mixture of cream cheese, yoghurt and lemon curd. Pop them in the fridge for half an hour to set, and then serve with a sprinkling of crushed-up ginger nut biscuits on top for an irresistible crunch.

Everyday Light ──────────────

Put the lemon and lime marmalade in a small bowl and stir with a dessertspoon until mostly smooth. It doesn't matter if there are a few small lumps. Divide the marmalade between the ramekin dishes and spread over the base of each in a thin layer.

Put the cream cheese in a small mixing bowl and mix until smooth with a wooden spoon. Add the lemon curd and mix it into the cream cheese until smooth. Add the yoghurt to the cream cheese mixture and mix until smooth.

Divide the mixture evenly among the ramekins, spread it over the marmalade and roughly smooth the top of each. Cover and place in the fridge to chill for a minimum of 30 minutes. These desserts should be soft and creamy after chilling.

When you are ready to serve, sprinkle the crushed ginger nut biscuit over the top of the desserts. Decorate each with a quarter of a lemon or lime slice. Serve alone or with churros or a crisp biscuit of your choice.

TIP:

You can use any crisp biscuit to crumble on the tops of these desserts. We think the flavour of ginger nut biscuits works well with lemon and lime, but it's up to you. Just remember to adjust the calories accordingly.

QUICK PREP

PEANUT BUTTER AND CHOCOLATE ICE POPS

🕐 **5 MINS**　　🍲 **NO COOK**　　✕ **MAKES 6**

* PLUS FREEZING OVERNIGHT

PER ICE POP:
92 KCAL / 11G CARBS

SPECIAL EQUIPMENT
6-hole ice-lolly mould
and 6 lolly sticks

400ml coconut plant-based
　drink
2 tbsp peanut butter powder
2 tbsp white granulated
　sweetener
3 tbsp fat free Greek yoghurt
20g dark chocolate, broken
　into pieces
10g roasted salted peanuts,
　crushed

How dreamy do chocolate-drizzled, peanut butter-flavoured lollies sound? There's no need to use your imagination with these slimming-friendly ice pops: simply combine coconut drink, peanut butter powder, fat-free yoghurt and sweetener to make a creamy mixture and let your freezer do the hard work for you. Coated in moreish crushed peanuts and drizzled with chocolate, they're at their best served with a side of sunshine!

Everyday Light

Put the coconut drink, peanut butter powder, sweetener and yoghurt in a mixing bowl or large jug and mix until smooth and combined.

Pour the mixture into 6 ice-lolly moulds. Don't overfill the moulds as the mixture will expand a little in the freezer. Add the lolly sticks and freeze overnight or until solid.

Add the chocolate to a small bowl and microwave in 10-second bursts and stir until melted.

Remove the ice pops from the freezer and remove them from the mould (you can dip the mould in hot water for a few seconds to help release the ice pops). Drizzle the ice pops with the melted chocolate and sprinkle over the crushed peanuts. Serve at once.

Quick PREP

↓

AIR FRYER and MULTI METHOD

FREEZE ME

BEFORE OR
AFTER COOKING

BATCH COOK

DAIRY FREE

GLUTEN FREE

ZINGER TUNA FISHCAKES

🕐 **20 MINS**　　🍲 **VARIABLE** (SEE BELOW)　　✕ **SERVES 4**

PER PORTION:
359 KCAL / 48G CARBS

FOR THE FISHCAKES
500g potatoes, peeled and cut
　　into chunks
low-calorie cooking spray
4 spring onions, trimmed and
　　finely chopped
1 garlic clove, peeled and
　　crushed
1 small red chilli, deseeded and
　　finely chopped
1 tsp paprika
2 x 110g tins tuna steak in a little
　　spring water, drained well and
　　flaked
2 ½ tbsp cornflour
1 medium egg, beaten
sea salt and freshly ground
　　black pepper

FOR THE COATING
80g Doritos Chilli Heatwave
　　flavour tortilla chips
2 tsp mild chilli powder
2 tsp garlic granules
2 tsp paprika
2 tsp onion granules

TO ACCOMPANY
75g mixed salad (+ 15 kcal per
　　serving)cooked serving)

If you're looking for ideas for how to use your store-cupboard tinned tuna, these spicy tuna fishcakes could hit the spot! We've livened things up, coating them in our popular Zinger crispy coating for a burst of chilli heat. We'd say they're medium hot, but tweak the chilli powder and fresh chilli to taste.

Everyday Light ——————————————————

OVEN METHOD
🍲 **45 MINUTES**

Put the potatoes in a saucepan of cold, salted water. Bring to the boil and cook for 15–20 minutes or until the potatoes are tender. Drain well and mash until smooth. Place in a medium bowl and set aside to become cool enough to handle.

Meanwhile, spray a small frying pan with low-calorie cooking spray and place over a medium-low heat. Add the spring onions, garlic, red chilli and paprika and cook gently for 2–3 minutes, until the onions have softened a little.

Preheat the oven to 200°C (fan 180°C/gas mark 6).

Put the Doritos, chilli powder, garlic granules, paprika and onion granules in a strong food bag. Squeeze out the air and seal the bag, then bash with a rolling pin or similar heavy object until the mixture resembles fine breadcrumbs. Tip the finely crushed mixture onto a plate and set aside.

Add the tuna, cooked spring onion, garlic, red chilli and paprika to the mashed potato in the bowl, season to taste and mix well. Divide the mixture into eight and shape into eight round fishcakes, each about 7cm (2¾in) in diameter and 2cm (¾in) thick.

Put the cornflour on a plate and the beaten egg on another plate. Dip the first fishcake into the cornflour and lightly dust on all sides, then dip the fishcake briefly into the egg to completely coat.

Continued...

QUICK PREP

TIP:
Floury potatoes such as
King Edwards are good
for mashing.

Dip the fishcake into the Zinger mix to coat on all sides and place on a plate. Repeat one at a time, until all eight fishcakes are fully coated, then place on a baking tray. Spray the tops of the fishcakes with low-calorie spray and bake in the oven for 10 minutes, then turn the fishcakes over using a fish slice and spray the other side with low-calorie cooking spray. Return to the oven and continue baking for a further 10–15 minutes, until crisp and piping hot throughout.

AIR-FRYER METHOD
🍲 **35 MINS**

SPECIAL EQUIPMENT
Air fryer

Put the potatoes in a saucepan of cold, salted water. Bring to the boil and cook for 15–20 minutes or until the potatoes are tender. Drain well and mash until smooth. Place in a medium bowl and set aside to become cool enough to handle.

Meanwhile, spray a small frying pan with low-calorie cooking spray and place over a medium-low heat. Add the spring onions, garlic, red chilli and paprika and cook gently for 2–3 minutes, until the onions have softened a little.

Preheat the air fryer for a few minutes at 170°C.

Put the Doritos, chilli powder, garlic granules, paprika and onion granules in a strong food bag. Squeeze out the air and seal the bag, then bash with a rolling pin or similar heavy object until the mixture resembles fine breadcrumbs. Tip the finely crushed mixture onto a plate and set aside.

Add the tuna, cooked spring onion, garlic, red chilli and paprika to the mashed potato in the bowl, season to taste and mix well. Divide the mixture into eight and shape into eight round fishcakes, each about 7cm (2¾in) in diameter and 2cm (¾in) thick.

Put the cornflour on a plate and the beaten egg on another plate. Dip the first fishcake into the cornflour and lightly dust on all sides, then dip the fishcake briefly into the egg to completely coat. Dip the fishcake into the Zinger mix to coat on all sides and place on a plate. Repeat one at a time, until all eight fishcakes are fully coated.

Place the fishcakes in the preheated air-fryer basket and spray with low-calorie cooking spray. You will probably need to cook the fishcakes in batches, depending on the capacity of your air fryer. Cook for 10–15 minutes, turning the fishcakes over halfway through. Spray again with low-calorie cooking spray and cook until crisp and piping hot throughout.

FREEZING INSTRUCTIONS FOR ALL METHODS
The fishcakes can be frozen before or after cooking. If freezing before cooking, open freeze on a tray, then layer between sheets of non-stick baking paper in a suitable freezerproof container. If freezing after cooking, layer between sheets of non-stick baking paper in a freezerproof container. Defrost cooked fishcakes in fridge and reheat in the air fryer at 170°C for 5–7 minutes, or in a 200°C (fan 180°C/gas mark 6) oven for about 15 minutes, until piping hot.

Serve with a crisp mixed salad, a drizzle of reduced-sugar sweet chilli sauce or a dollop of reduced-sugar-and-salt tomato ketchup or lighter-than-light mayonnaise.

> **TIP:**
> Use tuna steaks in spring water rather than tuna in oil. These tins of tuna hardly contain any spring water, so the tuna is almost dry and perfect for holding together in fishcakes. Tuna in oil will make the fishcakes too soft. If you use tinned tuna in brine or in a larger amount of spring water, make sure to drain well and squeeze out the excess liquid.

SMOKY CHICKEN AND BEAN STEW

🕐 **15 MINS**   🍲 **VARIABLE** (SEE BELOW)   ✕ **SERVES 4**

DAIRY FREE

GLUTEN FREE

USE GF STOCK CUBES AND HENDERSON'S RELISH

PER PORTION:
397 KCAL / 30G CARBS

low-calorie cooking spray
8 skinless, boneless chicken thighs (about 75g each) (visible fat removed)
3 smoked bacon medallions, cut into 1cm (½in) dice
1 medium onion, peeled and chopped
3 garlic cloves, peeled and crushed
2 medium carrots, peeled and cut into 1cm (½in)-thick slices
1 x 400g tin chopped tomatoes
1 x 415g tin reduced-sugar and reduced-salt baked beans in tomato sauce
1 large red roasted pepper in brine from a jar (about 130g), drained and diced
1 tbsp tomato puree
1 tbsp smoked paprika
1 tsp mild chilli powder
1 tsp dried thyme
1 tbsp Worcestershire sauce or Henderson's relish
1 low-salt chicken stock cube, crumbled
40g curly kale, shredded, weighed after any large stalks removed
sea salt and freshly ground black pepper

TO ACCOMPANY
80g steamed vegetables (+ 38 kcal per serving)

When it comes to wholesome home-cooked food, there's nothing quite like a stew. This is undeniably one of the best, with bacon and paprika turning the flavours up a notch, making sure every spoonful is rich, smoky and satisfying. The store-cupboard ingredients help keep costs down – and we've included 3 different methods, so that this recipe is ready on a timescale that suits you!

Weekly Indulgence ─────────────

OVEN METHOD
🍲 **1¾–2 HOURS**

SPECIAL EQUIPMENT
Large casserole dish (about 26cm/10¼in diameter)

Preheat the oven to 180°C (fan 160°C/gas mark 4).

Spray a large frying pan with low-calorie cooking spray and place over a medium heat. Add the chicken thighs and bacon and cook for 4–5 minutes until lightly browned on all sides, then transfer the chicken and bacon to the casserole dish.

Spray the large frying pan again with low-calorie cooking spray, add the onion, garlic and carrots and cook for about 10 minutes until the onion is softening and golden. Add to the chicken and bacon in the casserole dish. Add the chopped tomatoes, baked beans, roasted pepper, tomato puree, smoked paprika, chilli powder, thyme and Worcestershire sauce or Henderson's relish. Add the crumbled stock cube and stir well. Cover with a tight-fitting lid and bake in the oven for 1½–1¾ hours, until the chicken is cooked through, shows no sign of pinkness and the stew has thickened. Stir in the kale for the last 5 minutes of cooking, until wilted and tender. Check the stew towards the end of cooking and add a little water if needed.

Season with salt and pepper, if needed, and serve with steamed vegetables.

Continued...

AIR FRYER AND MULTI METHOD

SLOW-COOKER METHOD
🍲 4¼–5¼ HOURS

SPECIAL EQUIPMENT
Slow cooker

Spray a large frying pan with low-calorie cooking spray and place over a medium heat. Add the chicken thighs and bacon and cook for 4–5 minutes until lightly browned on all sides, then transfer the chicken and bacon to the slow cooker.

Spray the large frying pan again with low-calorie cooking spray, add the onion, garlic and carrots, and cook for about 10 minutes until the onion is softening and golden. Add to the chicken and bacon in the slow cooker. Add the chopped tomatoes, baked beans, roasted pepper, tomato puree, smoked paprika, chilli powder, thyme and Worcestershire sauce or Henderson's relish. Add the crumbled stock cube and stir well. Cover with the lid and cook on high for 4–5 hours, until the chicken is cooked through, shows no sign of pinkness and the stew has thickened. Stir in the kale for the last 5 minutes of cooking, until wilted and tender.

Season with salt and pepper, if needed, and serve with steamed vegetables.

INSTANT-POT METHOD
🍲 45 MINS

SPECIAL EQUIPMENT
Instant Pot

Spray the Instant Pot with low-calorie cooking spray and set to 'sauté'. Add the chicken thighs and bacon and cook for 4–5 minutes until lightly browned on all sides. Transfer to a plate and set aside.

Spray the Instant Pot again with low-calorie cooking spray, add the onion, garlic and carrots and cook for about 10 minutes, until the onion is softening and golden. Add the chicken and bacon to the vegetable mixture in the Instant Pot. Add the chopped tomatoes, baked beans, roasted pepper, tomato puree, smoked paprika, chilli powder, thyme and Worcestershire sauce or Henderson's relish to the Instant Pot. Add the crumbled stock cube and stir well. Cover with the lid and lock. Set the vent to 'sealing' and cook on high pressure for 30 minutes, until the chicken is cooked through, shows no sign of pinkness and the stew has thickened. Set the valve to 'venting' and release the pressure, taking care near the escaping steam.

Remove the lid and stir in the kale. Cook on 'sauté' for about 5 minutes until the kale has wilted and is tender. Season with salt and pepper, if needed. Serve with steamed vegetables.

> **TIP:**
> Use smoked paprika and smoked bacon medallions as they will give the stew a good smoky flavour.

PULLED PORK CHILLI

🕐 **20 MINS**   🍲 **VARIABLE** (SEE BELOW)   ✗ **SERVES 6**

PER PORTION:
267 KCAL /22G CARBS

SPECIAL EQUIPMENT
Casserole dish with tight-fitting lid, about 26cm (10¼in) in diameter, suitable for oven and hob

1 tbsp mild chilli powder
1 tsp ground cumin
1 tsp dried oregano
1 tsp smoked paprika
600g pork shoulder joint, weight after rind and all visible fat removed
low-calorie cooking spray
1 onion, peeled and sliced
3 garlic cloves, peeled and crushed
2 peppers (any colour), deseeded and sliced
2 carrots, peeled and diced
1 eating apple, peeled, cored and cut into small dice
1 x 400g tin chopped tomatoes
250ml / 100ml chicken or pork stock (1 chicken or pork stock cube dissolved in 250ml boiling water for oven method, 100ml for slow cooker method)
1 tbsp tomato puree
1 tbsp black treacle
1 x 400g tin black beans, drained and rinsed
juice of 1 lime

TO ACCOMPANY
60g wholemeal bread rolls (+ 146 kcal per roll) or 50g uncooked basmati rice per portion, cooked according to packet instructions (+ 173 kcal per 125g cooked serving)

Melt-in-the-mouth pulled pork takes this easy peasy chilli recipe to the next level. Made in the oven or slow cooker, you won't regret adding this to your midweek menu. Bulked out with vegetables and beans so the small joint of pork goes a long way, this one's great when you're watching your pennies as well as your calories. It's well worth batch-cooking and stashing away the leftovers for a rainy day.

Weekly Indulgence ─────────────

OVEN METHOD
🍲 **3 HOURS 15 MINS**

Preheat the oven to 160°C (fan 140°C/gas mark 3).

Mix the chilli powder, cumin, oregano and smoked paprika in a small bowl and use the spice mix to coat the pork joint on all sides.

Spray the casserole dish with low-calorie cooking spray and place over a medium heat. When hot, add the pork and cook for a minute or two on each side to seal the meat and toast the spices. Remove from the casserole dish and place to one side.

Give the casserole dish another spray with low-calorie cooking spray, add the onion and sauté for 5 minutes until starting to soften, then add the garlic and any remaining spice mix and cook for another minute. Add the peppers, carrots and apple then stir in the tomatoes, stock, tomato puree and treacle. Heat through, then place the pork back in the casserole dish and cover with a tight-fitting lid. Cook in the oven for 3 hours, checking occasionally from around the 2-hour mark: if it looks like it might be drying out, add a little extra water.

After 3 hours, remove from the oven. Remove the pork from the casserole dish. It should fall apart easily. Using two forks, shred the pork then return it to the casserole. Stir in the black beans and lime juice, cover and return to the oven for another 5 minutes for the beans to thoroughly heat through. Serve with rice.

The pork will keep in the fridge for up to 2 days. To freeze, follow standard guidelines for defrosting and reheating.

Continued...

SLOW-COOKER METHOD
🍲 HIGH: 6 HOURS LOW: 8 HOURS

SPECIAL EQUIPMENT
Slow cooker

Mix the chilli powder, cumin, oregano and smoked paprika in a small bowl and use the spice mix to coat the pork joint on all sides.

Spray a frying pan with low-calorie cooking spray and place over a medium heat. When hot, add the pork and cook for a minute or two on each side to seal the meat and toast the spices. Remove from the pan and place to one side.

Give the pan another spray with low-calorie cooking spray, add the onion and sauté for 5 minutes until starting to soften, then add the garlic and any remaining spice mix and cook for another minute.

Put the onion in the slow cooker pot and add the peppers, carrots and apple then stir in the tomatoes, stock, tomato puree and treacle. Place the pork on top, cover and cook for 5½ hours on high, 7½ hours on low.

After the required cooking time, check the pork. It should fall apart easily. Remove from the pot and shred with two forks. Return to the pot and stir in the black beans and lime juice. Replace the lid and cook for another 10–20 minutes, until the beans are thoroughly heated through. Serve!

The pork will keep in the fridge for up to 2 days. To freeze, follow standard guidelines for defrosting and reheating.

TIP:
Sealing and toasting the spices and sautéing the onion brings a wonderful depth of flavour to this chilli, but if you are short on time in the morning, you can just stir everything together in the slow cooker pot and turn it on. You'll still have a great-tasting dish at the end.

QUICK PREP

VEGGIE

VEGAN

USE PLANT-
BASED YOGHURT
AND MAPLE
OR AGAVE
SYRUP

FREEZE
ME

BURGERS ONLY

BATCH
COOK

DAIRY
FREE

USE PLANT-
BASED YOGHURT

GLUTEN
FREE

USE GF OATS
AND BREAD
ROLLS

LENTIL FALAFEL BURGERS

 🕐 **10 MINS**　🗑 **30 MINS**　✕ **SERVES 4**

PER PORTION:
355 KCAL /52G CARBS

SPECIAL EQUIPMENT
Food processor

FOR THE BURGERS
low-calorie cooking spray
40g rolled oats
2 x 400g tins green lentils, rinsed
　and drained
½ onion, peeled and chopped
40g baby spinach leaves
handful of fresh coriander
　leaves
handful of fresh parsley
handful of fresh mint leaves
2 tsp garlic granules
1 tsp ground cumin
1 tsp ground coriander
sea salt and freshly ground
　black pepper

FOR THE TZATZIKI
½ cucumber
150g fat-free Greek-style
　yoghurt
1–2 tsp harissa paste (to taste)
a few fresh mint leaves, finely
　chopped
1 tsp runny honey

TO SERVE
4 x 60g wholemeal rolls

TO ACCOMPANY
75g mixed salad
　(+ 15 kcal per serving)

There's no shortage of flavour in these veggie burgers! The patties, inspired by falafel, include blended lentils instead of chickpeas. Full of goodness (and budget friendly) they're crispy on the outside and soft inside, with a delicious herby taste. Our twist on tzatziki includes harissa and honey, so it's minty, spicy and slightly sweet all at once. Dollop it on your burger and get ready for the perfect bite!

Everyday Light

OVEN METHOD

SPECIAL EQUIPMENT
Food processor

Preheat the oven to 200°C (fan 180°C/gas mark 6) and spray a baking tray with low-calorie cooking spray. Place the oats in a food processor and blitz to a coarse flour. Remove and place to one side.

Pat the drained lentils with kitchen towel to remove any excess moisture, then put in the food processor with the onion, spinach, fresh herbs, garlic granules and spices. Blitz to a coarse paste – you don't want it completely smooth – then scrape into a bowl, add the blitzed oats and mix well. Taste and season with salt and pepper as needed.

Divide the falafel mix into 4 even-sized pieces and roll into balls, then flatten into burger shapes, each about 2cm (¾in) thick. Place on the greased baking tray, spray the tops with low-calorie cooking spray, and bake in the oven for 30 minutes, carefully flipping them halfway through, until golden brown and crisp on the outside.

While the burgers cook, make the tzatziki. Coarsely grate the cucumber and wrap it in a clean tea towel. Give it a good squeeze, to remove as much liquid as you can. This will stop the tzatziki from becoming watery. Put the cucumber into a mixing bowl and add the yoghurt, harissa paste, chopped mint, honey and a little salt and pepper to taste. Mix well.

When the burgers are cooked, split the wholemeal rolls in half and fill with the mixed salad. Place a burger on top and add a dollop of tzatziki. Serve!

Continued...

AIR FRYER AND MULTI METHOD

241

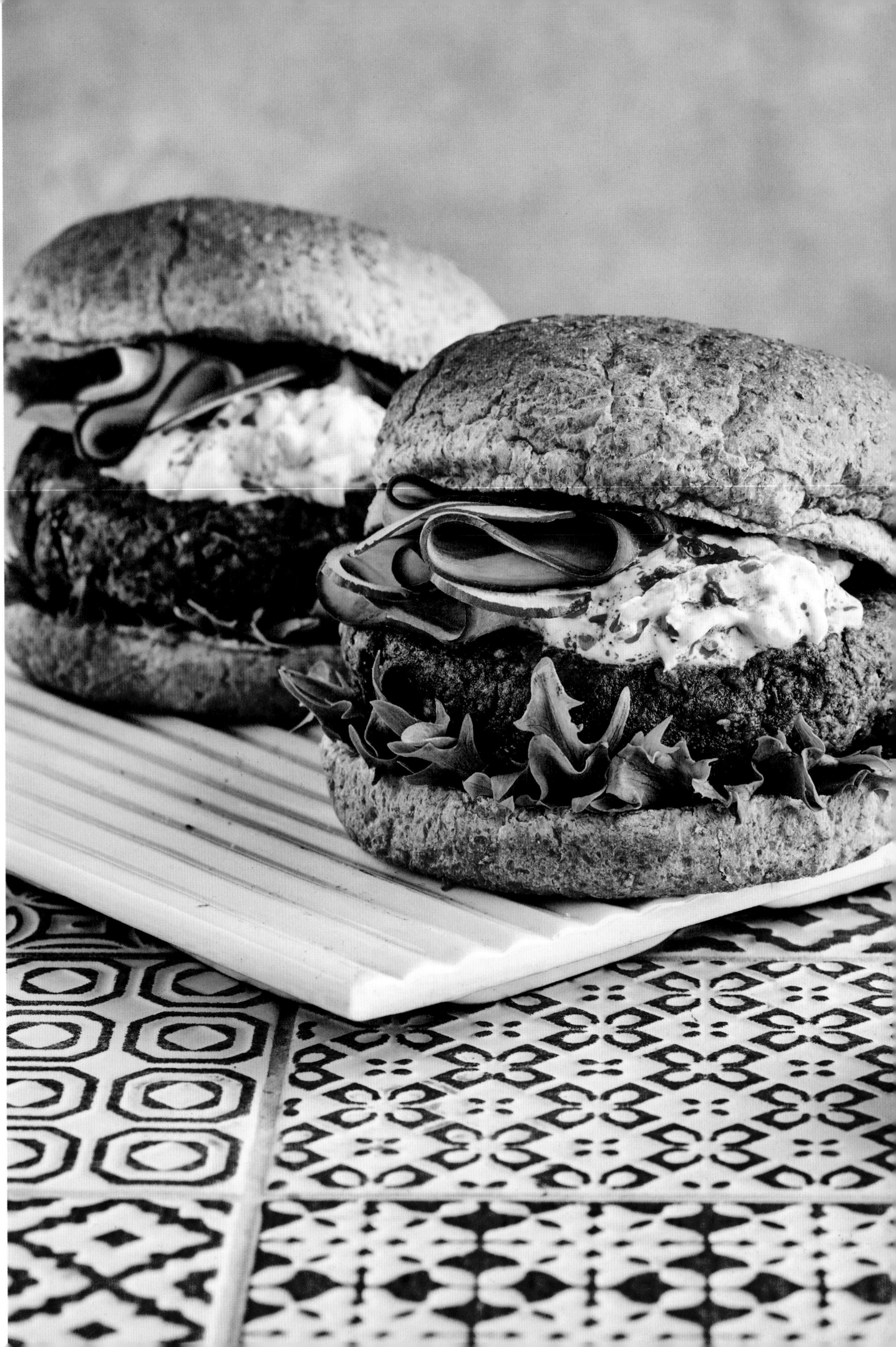

AIR-FRYER METHOD

SPECIAL EQUIPMENT
Food processor, air fryer

Place the oats in a food processor and blitz to a coarse flour. Remove and place to one side.

Pat the drained lentils with kitchen towel to remove any excess moisture, then put in the food processor with the onion, spinach, fresh herbs, garlic granules and spices. Blitz to a coarse paste – you don't want it completely smooth – then scrape into a bowl, add the blitzed oats and mix well. Taste and season with salt and pepper as needed. Divide the falafel mix into 4 even-sized pieces and roll into balls, then flatten into burger shapes, each about 2cm (¾in) thick.

Preheat the air fryer to 180°C. If your air fryer doesn't have a preheat function, turn it on and let it run for a few minutes to get to temperature.

Spray the burgers on both sides with low-calorie cooking spray and place in the air fryer. Cook for 15 minutes, carefully flipping them halfway through, until golden brown and crisp on the outside.

While the burgers cook, make the tzatziki. Coarsely grate the cucumber and wrap it in a clean tea towel. Give it a good squeeze, to remove as much liquid as you can. This will stop the tzatziki from becoming watery. Put the cucumber into a mixing bowl and add the yoghurt, harissa paste, chopped mint, honey and a little salt and pepper to taste. Mix well.

When the burgers are cooked, split the wholemeal rolls in half and fill with the mixed salad. Place a burger on top and add a dollop of tzatziki. Serve!

INDEX

Page references in *italics* indicate images.

NUTRITIONAL INFO PER SERVING

Quick COOK

BREAKFAST	ENERGY KJ/KCAL	FAT (G)	SATURATED FAT (G)	CARBS (G)	SUGAR (G)	FIBRE (G)	PROTEIN (G)	SALT (G)
BREAKFAST TACOS	1364/326	14	4	27	5.7	5.9	20	0.95
POACHED EGG WITH CRISPY PARMA HAM	1083/259	12	4.6	15	4.4	2	22	2.3
GREEN EGGS AND HAM	1653/396	21	7	20	3.5	5.3	30	2.5
SAVOURY BREAKFAST PANCAKES	1665/396	13	3.6	43	6	3.5	25	1.9

FAKEAWAYS	ENERGY KJ/KCAL	FAT (G)	SATURATED FAT (G)	CARBS (G)	SUGAR (G)	FIBRE (G)	PROTEIN (G)	SALT (G)
TERIYAKI CHICKEN DONBURI	1558/368	0.8	0.2	51	3.5	3.9	15	0.4
BEEF AND PINEAPPLE BURGERS	1407/335	12	4.2	33	11	2.9	22	0.83
SZECHUAN-STYLE NOODLES	1701/403	7.2	1.5	47	7.3	4.1	36	7.1
CASHEW NUT CHICKEN	1150/274	11	2.2	19	10	2.8	22	2
CHILLI CRAB LINGUINE	1570/371	3.4	0.9	58	7.5	5.8	24	1.2
GREEN VEG PASTA	1185/281	5.2	2.5	40	5.6	5.1	15	0.58
MEATBALLS WITH GINGER AND SPRING ONION	1277/303	7.6	2.7	24	15	1.7	31	5.1
GARLICKY SURF AND TURF	1437/341	11	4.5	1.9	1.3	0	59	2.1
TAMARIND CHICKEN	1171/279	9.3	6.7	13	8.2	3.4	34	2.8
BEEF WITH CHILLI AND GARLIC	1194/284	8.2	3.2	10	6.3	2.2	41	3.1
BOURBON GLAZED CHICKEN	997/236	1.9	0.5	12	11	0.5	34	1.5
HAM, CHEESE AND SPINACH OMELETTE WRAP	1543/368	16	6.5	25	3.6	3.1	29	2.1
YELLOW THAI-STYLE CURRY	1313/311	5.2	1.5	21	11	6.4	42	2.7
BEEF, GINGER AND ORANGE STIR-FRY	1124/266	5	1.8	28	20	3.6	26	2.8
GARLIC, CHILLI AND PARSLEY SPAGHETTI	1400/332	6.2	3.1	52	2.9	3.9	15	0.4

SOUPS AND STEWS	ENERGY KJ/KCAL	FAT (G)	SATURATED FAT (G)	CARBS (G)	SUGAR (G)	FIBRE (G)	PROTEIN (G)	SALT (G)
CARROT AND GINGER SOUP	510/122	1.9	0.2	19	17	8.7	2.3	3
PEANUT RAMEN	1280/304	6.4	2.2	38	14	10	18	5.9

BAKES, ROASTS AND ONE POTS	ENERGY KJ/KCAL	FAT (G)	SATURATED FAT (G)	CARBS (G)	SUGAR (G)	FIBRE (G)	PROTEIN (G)	SALT (G)
PIZZA POCKETS	705/167	4.6	1.7	23	3.7	1.6	7.8	0.64
CAULIFLOWER CHEESE WITH BACON	1212/288	8.1	3.2	28	11	3	26	3.9
PIZZA PORK	1206/288	15	6.1	4.6	3.6	1	32	0.99

SNACK AND SIDES	ENERGY KJ/KCAL	FAT (G)	SATURATED FAT (G)	CARBS (G)	SUGAR (G)	FIBRE (G)	PROTEIN (G)	SALT (G)
TUNA MELT WRAP	552/131	3.6	2.1	12	2	1.7	12	0.73
ROASTED LEMON AND PARMESAN BROCCOLI	239/57	2.2	1.1	3	1.5	3	5.1	0.23
STICKY PINEAPPLE FRIED RICE	1512/358	5	1	66	17	6.7	8.9	4
TUNA BEAN SALAD	403/96	1.2	0.3	10	2.5	3	9.5	0.6
BACON, CHEESE AND TOMATO SLICES	608/145	7.5	3.5	12	1	1	7.3	0.66

SWEET TREATS	ENERGY KJ/KCAL	FAT (G)	SATURATED FAT (G)	CARBS (G)	SUGAR (G)	FIBRE (G)	PROTEIN (G)	SALT (G)
BLACK FOREST BAKEWELLS	335/80	3	0.9	12	1.3	0.5	2	0.18
APRICOT DANISH-STYLE PASTRIES	493/118	5	2.1	15	1.1	1.1	2.4	0.15
PEACH BELLINI JELLIES	629/150	0	0	20	13	2.7	0.8	0.04
BANANA PANCAKE TRAYBAKE	589/139	2.1	0.8	26	5.1	1.2	4.6	0.43
RASPBERRY FILO TART	708/168	3.9	1.05	26	8	3.45	5	0.4

AIR FRYER AND MULTI METHOD	ENERGY KJ/KCAL	FAT (G)	SATURATED FAT (G)	CARBS (G)	SUGAR (G)	FIBRE (G)	PROTEIN (G)	SALT (G)
ZINGER HALLOUMI FRIES WITH GARLIC AND ONION DIP	1292/308	14	6.8	25	4.2	2.3	19	2.1
SWEET CHILLI CHICKEN NUGGETS	881/208	3.4	0.8	14	6.2	2.1	29	1.2
PESTO CHICKEN ESCALOPE	1167/277	7.4	1.1	17	1.2	0.5	35	0.62
FIERY CHILLI CHICKEN KEBABS	816/193	38	1.1	12	12	0.8	27	1.8
CHICKEN PARMO	1909/452	11	4.6	37	4.5	0.7	51	1.5
CRISPY GARLIC MUSHROOMS	601/144	8	0.9	14	1.7	0.5	4.7	0.45
MASHED POTATO BALLS	700/166	3.8	1.6	23	1.5	1.8	9.4	0.76
MOCHA LAVA MUG CAKES	995/239	16	5.9	19	4.1	2.4	6.5	0.49

Quick PREP

BREAKFAST	ENERGY KJ/KCAL	FAT (G)	SATURATED FAT (G)	CARBS (G)	SUGAR (G)	FIBRE (G)	PROTEIN (G)	SALT (G)
BREAKFAST FOLDED WRAP	1290/307	7.6	2.2	33	6.6	7.5	23	1.9
BANANA AND BLUEBERRY MUFFINS	789/188	6.5	2.2	30	4.5	1.3	4.7	0.39
EGG AND BACON PIES	690/165	7.2	1.9	12	2.6	0.9	12	0.88

FAKEAWAYS	ENERGY KJ/KCAL	FAT (G)	SATURATED FAT (G)	CARBS (G)	SUGAR (G)	FIBRE (G)	PROTEIN (G)	SALT (G)
SWEET AND SOUR HALLOUMI CURRY	1381/329	12	6.8	30	14	6.1	23	3.1
TOFU AND COCONUT CURRY	1192/285	15	7.3	18	9.4	6.1	16	1.3
LOADED PUPPY FRIES	1599/381	12	3.3	44	7.6	6	20	1.4
FRAGRANT CHICKEN CURRY	1344/321	12	1.1	21	8.5	6.4	29	2.2
LEMON AND GINGER CHICKEN	987/233	2.2	0.4	19	13	1.6	33	2.2
PERI-PERI PULLED CHICKEN WRAPS	1124/267	4.9	0.8	30	9.4	5.5	21	0.6
CREAMY CHIPOTLE BEEF	1031/245	7.7	2.9	10	8.5	2.7	32	1.4

	ENERGY KJ/KCAL	FAT (G)	SATURATED FAT (G)	CARBS (G)	SUGAR (G)	FIBRE (G)	PROTEIN (G)	SALT (G)
SHREDDED VEGETABLE AND CHICKEN SALAD	788/187	3.1	0.5	11	9.8	4.2	26	1.3
SAUSAGE AND TOMATO MAC AND CHEESE	2028/482	15	6.9	58	11	4.3	25	1.4
SALT 'N' PEPPER CHICKEN SALAD	1493/354	5.6	1.1	40	19	5	35	5.3
MUSHROOM KEEMA	759/180	2.4	0.3	28	14	6.8	7.1	1.7

SOUPS AND STEWS	ENERGY KJ/KCAL	FAT (G)	SATURATED FAT (G)	CARBS (G)	SUGAR (G)	FIBRE (G)	PROTEIN (G)	SALT (G)
BACON AND RED PESTO SOUP	1225/292	12	1.8	30	6.9	4.2	13	4
CULLEN SKINK	1040/246	1.4	0.4	33	9.2	4.2	23	1.1
ROASTED ROOT VEGETABLE SOUP	504/120	1.8	0.1	19	11	6.2	3.3	2.3
SPICY PASTA SOUP	1157/274	3.2	0.3	44	16	10	11	2.7
CREAMY BACON AND BUTTERNUT SQUASH CHICKEN	1174/278	6.2	1.8	15	9.3	2.9	40	2.3

BAKES, ROASTS AND ONE POTS	ENERGY KJ/KCAL	FAT (G)	SATURATED FAT (G)	CARBS (G)	SUGAR (G)	FIBRE (G)	PROTEIN (G)	SALT (G)
TOMATO AND MANGO SALSA CHICKEN	982/232	4.1	1.9	12	11	1.5	35	0.52
CHEESY MARMITE PASTA BAKE	2103/499	13	6.1	57	7.7	5.5	35	2.6
HAM AND LEEK GRATIN	1561/373	16	7.8	28	9.8	4.2	26	2
SPANISH-STYLE ROAST VEGETABLES	576/137	2	0.4	19	15	8	5.8	0.29
BBQ BOLOGNESE	1193/284	8.1	3.1	19	15	5.5	30	3.1
CHICKEN PUTTANESCA BAKE	1121/265	4.5	1.4	13	11	3.8	40	0.92
CREAMY SAUSAGE AND MASH PIE	1683/400	8.8	3.3	50	15	8.8	26	2.7
APPLE AND MUSTARD SWINEHERD'S PIE	1819/431	7.1	2.5	53	15	9.3	34	0.65
STICKY PLUM AND CHICKEN TRAYBAKE	1397/331	6.9	1.9	15	13	2	51	0.56
CHIMICHURRI BAKED COD	759/179	1.5	0.3	15	3.8	3.3	24	0.42
BOBOTIE	1315/313	10	3.7	21	16	3.5	33	1.1
DIJON SAUSAGES	1208/288	11	3.6	19	9.4	4.9	26	3.1

CURRIED QUICHE	776/186	11	6.3	8.1	6.7	0.8	13	0.73
CREAMY HUNTER'S CHICKEN	1493/354	5.6	1.1	40	19	5	35	5.3
CIDER CHICKEN PIE	1385/328	3.5	1.4	35	7	4.5	34	1.1
CHEESY GARLIC GAMMON	1444/344	12	6	9.3	6.5	2.4	49	5.1
ROASTED RED PEPPER CHICKEN	1587/376	8	4.5	27	23	4.3	44	1.9
MARGHERITA COD	934/222	6.2	3.4	8.4	7.4	2.1	31	0.79

SNACK AND SIDES	ENERGY KJ/KCAL	FAT (G)	SATURATED FAT (G)	CARBS (G)	SUGAR (G)	FIBRE (G)	PROTEIN (G)	SALT (G)
ROAST PORK AND APPLE SALAD	839/199	5.5	1.6	15	14	2.9	21	0.55
BOULANGERE POTATOES	893/211	0.9	0.1	42	6.5	5.8	5.2	1.3
SWEET POTATO HASH BROWNS	237/56	1	0.3	9.7	2.4	1	0.6	0.38
SWEET CARROT AND GINGER SLAW	291/69	0.5	0	13	13	2.7	0.5	0.41
PRAWN SAGANAKI	876/208	6.7	3.9	8.4	7.9	2.2	26	2.1

SWEET TREATS	ENERGY KJ/KCAL	FAT (G)	SATURATED FAT (G)	CARBS (G)	SUGAR (G)	FIBRE (G)	PROTEIN (G)	SALT (G)
WINTER BERRY COBBLER	1134/270	6.8	2	51	13	6	5.7	0.26
BISCOFF SPONGE TRAYBAKE	530/127	7.7	2.3	14	5	0.5	1.7	0.27
ORANGE AND GINGER RHUBARB CRUMBLE	1208/289	10	3.3	46	2.2	5.5	4.9	0.25
CARAMEL APPLE UPSIDE-DOWN CAKE	955/229	12	3.8	29	13	1.2	3.3	0.49
COOKIES AND CREAM CHEESECAKE	1113/266	12	5.3	28	15	1.3	12	0.78
CHOCOLATE SPONGE TRAYBAKE	462/111	5.9	2.1	13	3.5	0.5	2.8	0.29
MINT CHOCOLATE MOUSSE	614/148	13	10	6.5	6.1	0.5	2	0.18
CHOCOLATE AND GINGER TART	1317/314	13	5.6	44	21	1.5	6.6	0.49
RASPBERRY SORBET	437/104	0.5	0.1	17	16	9.5	1.5	0.04

	ENERGY KJ/KCAL	FAT (G)	SATURATED FAT (G)	CARBS (G)	SUGAR (G)	FIBRE (G)	PROTEIN (G)	SALT (G)
SALTED CARAMEL FROYO	620/146	0.9	0.6	21	12	0.6	13	0.94
LEMON AND LIME POTS	674/159	2	1	27	25	0	8.5	0.29
PEANUT BUTTER AND CHOCOLATE ICE POPS	385/92	3.5	1.6	11	3.7	1.6	5.7	0.26

AIR FRYER AND MULTI METHOD	ENERGY KJ/KCAL	FAT (G)	SATURATED FAT (G)	CARBS (G)	SUGAR (G)	FIBRE (G)	PROTEIN (G)	SALT (G)
ZINGER TUNA FISHCAKES	1513/359	7.5	1.2	48	4.3	5.8	22	1
SMOKY CHICKEN AND BEAN STEW	1672/397	7.4	1.7	30	18	10	46	2.5
PULLED PORK CHILLI	1125/267	6	1.6	22	17	8.1	27	27
LENTIL FALAFEL BURGERS	1499/355	4.8	0.8	52	7.5	11	11	0.85

ACKNOWLEDGEMENTS

As ever, we owe a huge thank you to so many people who work so hard to bring this book together. We really appreciate you all and can't thank you enough for the time and effort you put into making this book something we are hugely proud of.

Thank you to our publisher Carole Tonkinson. To Martha Burley, Bríd Enright, Jodie Lancet-Grant, Katy Denny, Alenka Oblak and the rest of the team at Bluebird for helping us create this book and believing in Pinch of Nom throughout this journey. Major thanks also to our agent Clare Hulton for your unwavering support and guidance.

To Mike English for the amazing photos and to Kate Wesson for making our food look so, so good and to Kristine Jakobsson, Federica Cerniglia and Max Robinson for all your assistance. Big thanks go out to Emma Wells, Nikki Dupin and Beth Free at Nic & Lou for making this book so beautiful!

We also want to thank our friends and family who have made this book possible.

Special thanks go to Laura Davis and Katie Mitchell for the endless hours you've put into this and for working so hard to get things right!

A huge thank you to our wonderful team of recipe developers who work tirelessly to help us bring these recipes to life; Lisa Allinson, Sharon Fitzpatrick and Holly Levell.

Massive thanks also go to Sophie Fryer, Hannah Cutting, Nick Nicolaou, Rosie Sparrow, Ellie Drinkwater and Laura Valentine for your writing and marketing support. To Cate Meadows and Jacob Lathbury for your creative and visual genius.

Additional thanks to Matthew Maney, Jessica Molyneux, Rubi Bourne, Vince Bourne, Cheryl Lloyd and Sarah Maney for supporting us and the business – we are so proud to work alongside you all.

We also want to thank our friends and family who have made this book possible. A very big thank you to Dr Hannah Cowan, Helen Child Villiers, Katie McKenna, Nicola Brooks, Emma Brooks & Jayne Dawson. Your support has meant the world.

To our wonderful moderators and online support team; thank you for all your hard work keeping the peace and for all your support.

Furry thanks to Mildred, Wanda, Ginger Cat, Freda and Brandi for the daily moments of joy.

And finally . . . Huge thanks go to Paul Allinson for your unwavering support. And to Cath Allinson who is never forgotten.

ABOUT THE AUTHORS
KATE *and* KAY

FOUNDERS OF PINCH OF NOM
www.pinchofnom.com

Kate and Kay Allinson owned a restaurant together on the Wirral, where Kate was head chef. Together they created the Pinch of Nom blog with the aim of teaching people how to cook. They began sharing healthy, slimming recipes and today Pinch of Nom is the UK's most-visited food blog with an active and engaged online community of over 4 million followers.

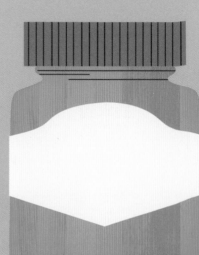

Easy recipes that are tasty and filling

BETHANY

Quick and easy and delicious!

MARY

All of the taste without all of the calories

ANNMARIE

It's really helped grow my confidence in cooking!

TRACEY